Marty Mann's

NEW PRIMER ON ALCOHOLISM

Marty Mann's

NEW
PRIMER
ON
ALCOHOLISM

How People Drink,

How To Recognize Alcoholics,
and

What To Do About Them

HOLT, RINEHART AND WINSTON

New York   Chicago   San Francisco

612.01446
copy 4

To all those men and women of A.A. and NCA whose contributions have helped alcoholics, and with particular gratitude and affection to:

DR. HARRY M. TIEBOUT

BILL AND LOIS

DR. RUTH FOX

DR. E. M. JELLINEK

YVELIN GARDNER *and* R. BRINKLEY SMITHERS

Contents

Preface   ix

Preface to the First Edition   xi

1. *ALCOHOLISM AND ITS CAUSES*   3

2. *WHAT IS AN ALCOHOLIC?*   17

3. *WHO IS AN ALCOHOLIC?*   63

4. *WHO IS NOT AN ALCOHOLIC?*   78

5. *HOW CAN I BE SURE THAT X IS*

      REALLY AN ALCOHOLIC?   94

6. *THE "HOME TREATMENT"*   102

7. *ALCOHOLICS CAN RECOVER*   109

8. *THE ROAD TO RECOVERY*   118

9. *ALCOHOLISM INFORMATION*

      CENTERS   128

10. *TREATMENT*   136

viii   *Contents*

11. *ALCOHOLICS ANONYMOUS* 163

12. *A RESOURCE FOR EVERYONE: NCA* 188

13. *WHAT TO DO ABOUT AN*

 ALCOHOLIC 196

14. *WHAT THE ALCOHOLIC CAN DO*

 HIMSELF 225

15. *LET'S GO!* 233

 Selected Bibliography 237

PREFACE

The original Primer has been almost entirely re-written to create this New Primer. Only the basic facts about alcoholism and its symptoms remain unchanged. Yet even here some new insights have been added which should make it easier to recognize, and to accept, alcoholism for what it is: a vicious and progressive disease which nevertheless can be successfully treated.

There have been, since the original Primer was published, tremendous and important advances in this field in both treatment and the availability of services. This made it essential to bring the book up to date if its usefulness was to continue unimpaired.

Hundreds of face-to-face meetings with men and women who found their way to help through the original Primer have convinced me of the great and continuing need for such a book, and of the urgency of keeping its practical information current.

Alcoholism is coming into its own at long last. The climate of thinking about it has changed radically. New attitudes are producing definite action. Alcoholism programs are springing up everywhere: in communities through voluntary citizens' groups; in states through legislation; in churches, and schools, in industry, and in organized labor. The pace of the forward movement is almost a breakneck one, as if to make up for lost time.

There is no time to lose, for the number of people who fall victim to alcoholism continues to rise. The estimate for 1955 was 4,712,000.* Five millions would be a fair figure for 1958. And that means twenty-five million nonalcoholics directly affected: a grand total that involves over one sixth of our population with alcoholism.

Too many in this great mass of people still do not know the facts about alcoholism, or what to do about it. Too many are still hiding, in fear and shame. It is for them I write, to bring them the latest news—the good news about things *that work*.

If in this way more alcoholics can be returned to healthy happy useful lives, I shall be well rewarded.

MARTY MANN

New York, March, 1958.

---

* "Alcoholism: Nature and Extent of the Problem," Mark Keller, *The Annals of the American Academy of Political and Social Science*, Jan. 1958, p. 6.

PREFACE TO THE FIRST EDITION

This book is written to fill a great need; a terrible and urgent need for practical, usable information on alcoholism and alcoholics. Much has been written in the last ten years on alcoholism, but a large part of this writing has been scientific and technical. That part which has been of immediate practical use has been addressed primarily to the alcoholic himself, rather than to the far greater number of people who have to cope with the alcoholic: families, friends, neighbors, employers (and employees), fellow workers, etc., etc.

It has been estimated by competent authorities* that there are some 4,000,000 alcoholics in the United States. This means that there are probably 20,000,000 people, nonalcoholics among whom these alcoholics live and have their being, who are more or less seriously affected by the

---

* Section on Alcohol Studies, Laboratory of Applied Physiology, Yale University, New Haven, Conn.

alcoholics' behavior. The alcoholic does not live in a vacuum. Other people, therefore, are bound to suffer from the effects of the disease which afflicts the alcoholic. Too often they suffer helplessly, unable to do anything whatever about it, since it is not their own illness. But there is much they can do, even so. They need not be helpless if they have knowledge. And the knowledge exists; it needs only to become widely known, and to be used.

This book is intended to fill the gap in our existing literature on alcoholism: to provide the nonalcoholic world in which the alcoholic lives with practical, usable information which has proved its value; in short, which works. It is not intended as a scientific treatise, nor will it attempt scientific definitions. Purely scientific terminology will be avoided as much as possible, in favor of terms which are already in common use, with their meanings generally understood and accepted. Where no such terms exist, words or phrases which are self-explanatory will be used. There are exceptions, of course, where quotations are taken from scientific papers; and there are a good number of these, for science has made great strides in this field in recent years, even though it has not yet found all the answers regarding the true nature of alcoholism, its causes, or its cure.

Nevertheless, despite the undoubted gaps in our scientific knowledge; despite the special pleading of certain groups (such as the so-called "temperance" groups) that there is only one answer to alcoholism—their own; the facts tell a hopeful story of many answers, many different solutions. The evidence supports this hope, with the proof of many thousands of existing recoveries from alcoholism.

It is my belief that millions more alcoholics could recover if they and those surrounding them had, and used, the basic knowledge and the practical information which we already possess. In the fervent hope that this may come to pass, I offer this book.

MARTY MANN

New York, April, 1950.

Marty Mann's

NEW PRIMER ON ALCOHOLISM

1
ALCOHOLISM AND ITS CAUSES

Alcoholism is a disease which manifests itself chiefly by the uncontrollable drinking of the victim, who is known as an alcoholic. It is a progressive disease, which, if left untreated, grows more virulent year by year, driving its victims further and further from the normal world, and deeper and deeper into an abyss which has only two outlets: insanity or death. Alcoholism, therefore, is a progressive, and often a fatal, disease . . . *if* it is not treated and arrested. But it can be arrested.

Today there exist a number of successful treatments for alcoholism. The fellowship known as Alcoholics Anonymous has helped thousands of alcoholics to recover, and many others have been restored to a normal, useful life through other methods of treatment. It is no longer a hopeless condition, provided it is recognized and treated. Recognition of the true nature of alcoholism and the need for treating it, is, however, the essential first step.

The statement that alcoholism is a disease has pro-

?

voked widespread discussion during recent years. It has been asserted, questioned, debated, denied and defended. On the whole, it has been accepted. Furthermore, that acceptance has grown and spread through every segment of the population.

It has been featured, and printed as front-page news by newspapers all over the country, hailed, in effect, as a brand-new discovery. It has come as a revelation to thousands of alcoholics seeking desperately to find a reason for their, to them, inexplicable drinking behavior; and for many of them it has been the greatest single factor leading to eventual recovery from that disease. It has come as healing balm to the tortured hearts of wives, mothers and husbands of alcoholics, who had hopelessly clung to a lonely belief that *their* alcoholic wasn't the "bad character" of general opinion, but had "something" specifically wrong with him that drove him to destructive excess in drinking. Finally, it has come as a constructive tool to the hands of baffled and frustrated would-be helpers, both professional and lay people whose work or inclination led them to deal with alcoholics.

Curiously enough, in view of the tremendous importance of this knowledge, it is not a new discovery. The concept of alcoholism as a disease has been on the scientific record for a very long time, and has been rediscovered over and over again by observant medical men and laymen alike. What is it that they have observed? Simply this: most alcoholics show a pattern of symptoms, particularly behavior symptoms, which are strikingly similar. Today, when physicians and scientists observe such a pattern repeating itself with only minor variations in a great variety of individuals, they call it a syndrome[1] and give it a name. It then enters the roster of identifiable diseases.

"The Syndrome of Alcohol Addiction" is the title of a scientific paper on alcoholism published some years ago.[2] But this is only one recent addition to a long history of specific statements by qualified writers, researchers, and observers. Volume 1, No. 1 (June, 1940) of the *Quarterly Journal of Studies on Alcohol,* America's only scientific journal on the subject, carries the following statement:

Many writers on inebriety have been credited with recognizing, for the first time, alcohol addiction as a disease. Earlier and earlier instances are mentioned in historical notes and perhaps the original coiner of the phrase will never be ascertained. Certainly Dr. Thomas Trotter was not the first writer to assert this, as a few years before him Benjamin Rush had referred to alcohol addiction as a disease. On the other hand, it was probably Trotter who was the first to go farther than merely stating the fact and who actually dealt with the question in a truly medical sense.

Dr. Benjamin Rush, foremost medical practitioner and teacher of his time, minced no words in his declaration. His scientific paper, entitled "An Inquiry into the Effects of Ardent Spirits upon the Human Body and Mind with an Account of the Means of Preventing and

---

[1] SYNDROME: (concurrence)—is a term applied to a group of symptoms occurring together regularly and thus constituting a disease to which some particular name is given . . . BLACK'S MEDICAL DICTIONARY, 1948.

[2] "The Syndrome of Alcohol Addiction," Harry M. Tiebout, M.D. *Quarterly Journal of Studies on Alcohol,* March, 1945.

of the Remedies for Curing Them" was published in 1785. After a brief preamble he writes, "I shall begin by briefly describing their [ardent spirits'] prompt, or immediate effects, in a fit of drunkenness. This odious disease (for by that name it should be called) appears with more or less of the following symptoms . . ."

Dr. Thomas Trotter received his medical degree from the University of Edinburgh in 1788. The paper which he submitted as his doctor's thesis was entitled "Essay, Medical, Philosophical and Chemical, on Drunkenness," and caused such a stir that he received the thanks of the Royal Humane Society for his work. His definition of alcoholism goes as follows: "In medical language, I consider drunkenness, strictly speaking, to be a disease; produced by a remote cause, and giving birth to actions and movements in the living body, that disorder the functions of health."

In 1830 a report was issued by "The Committee of the Connecticut Medical Society, to inquire whether it is expedient and practicable to establish an institution for the reformation [sic!] of intemperate persons." This report, which not only called for such an institution, stressing the failure of the current method of sending alcoholics to jail or workhouse, also stated: "Before attempting to eradicate any *disease* [the italics are mine, M. M.], we should endeavor to investigate its character, to inquire into its nature and tendency, and ascertain as far as practicable, the impediments which exist to its removal." In short, research into causes, effects and treament of alcoholism.

During the next hundred years there were many

more such reports—official, medical and lay. Most of them accepted the concept of alcoholism as a disease, as their fundamental basis, but that concept never seemed to penetrate beyond the immediate circle of hearers or readers of the papers or reports. Somehow it never reached the general public, the very place where alcoholism flourished and took its appalling toll. The public, including the countless alcoholics who were, and are, a part of the general population, were apparently without the slightest hint that any concept whatever had been developed about alcoholism, or even that it had finally acquired such a name. "Habitual drunkenness" was the name in current use up to a very few years ago, and the victim was called, simply, "a drunkard." Implied in those two names was all the contempt and opprobrium usually reserved for robbers of poor widows or defilers of the young.

"Drunkenness" or "habitual drunkenness" were, however, the terms used by all of the early writers on the subject, for the term "alcoholism" had not then been invented. Today the word "drunkenness" is considered too broad a term, for it is recognized that many people voluntarily set out to get drunk, more or less frequently, without necessarily being victims of the disease of alcoholism. This recognition is not general, however, and needs to be much more widely understood; for many people, through ignorance, still confuse the heavy drinker and the "occasional drunk" with the sick alcoholic.

The distinction was once made very clearly by no less a personage than Seneca, who lived from 4 B.C. to 63 A.D., and who wrote in his *Epistolae Morales:*

Posidonius maintains that the word "drunken" is used two ways,—in the one case of a man who is loaded with wine and has no control over himself; in the other of a man who is accustomed to get drunk, and is a slave to the habit. . . . You will surely admit that there is a great difference between a man who is drunk and a drunkard. He who is actually drunk may be in this state for the first time and may not have the habit, [and] the drunkard is often free from drunkenness.

Heavy drinking and its connotations will be fully dealt with in a later chapter. Here it is sufficient to say that the heavy drinker who drinks to drunkenness usually does so quite casually, *and by choice;* although he may, at times, inadvertently exceed even his own broad limitations; and often may regret his excesses the morning after. For him, however, this is not too serious a matter, and he will still choose to "get good and drunk" another time.

The "occasional drunk" is closely akin to the heavy drinker, except that his drinking bouts are apt to be prolonged into real sprees, which occur at chosen intervals. The "occasional drunk" would deeply resent having any such opprobrious term applied to him, if one did it to his face, and with good enough reason. Such drinkers get drunk, or, as they would express it "tight" or "high," or, sometimes, "stinko," entirely by choice and with malice aforethought, at times and on occasions selected by them as appropriate for such behavior. And in our culture, such occasions do indeed occur with some frequency, especially in certain urban circles. Their manner of drinking, and the amounts they consume, are quite acceptable in some sections of our society. Whether or not this is a fortunate situation is not a matter for discussion here.

The key word in both these descriptions is "choice," and this is the vital difference between the heavy drinker and the "occasional drunk" (who, like the alcoholic, may get in trouble, in the news, the courts, the jail or the hospital, as the result of a drinking bout), and the true alcoholic. The alcoholic, who is also aptly known as a "compulsive drinker," *does not choose.* He has lost the power of choice in the matter of drinking, and that is precisely the nature of his disease, alcoholism.

The victims of alcoholism only rarely set out to get drunk. Usually they wish simply to enjoy a few drinks "like other people." This, they find to their horror and dismay, does not seem possible for them; almost every time they drink they end up drunk, entirely against their will and intention. At a later stage of their progressive illness, they find matters even worse, for by then they frequently determine not to drink at all, only to find themselves, again to their own horror and dismay, drinking once more to drunkenness in total contradiction to their expressed will in the matter. With alcoholics, choice is no longer possible, whether to drink or not to drink, or of the amount consumed, or the effects of that amount upon them, or the occasions upon which drunkenness occurs.

It is true that with many alcoholics, even in the advanced stages of alcoholism, there are occasions now and then when their power of choice and restraint seems miraculously returned to them. They have memorable evenings when they are able to drink along with (and no more than) the company they are in; memorable days when daylong nipping is negligible and seems to have no untoward effect; memorable periods when for a few days they seem to need no more than the normal nonalcoholic regular drinker takes; even thrice-memorable times when they can consume their usual excessive amount and not show it.

This, unfortunately, is one of the least-understood peculiarities of the still baffling disease of alcoholism. The fact that this consistently recurs is known to all alcoholics, who are consistently fooled by it into thinking —and hoping—that after all they are just like other drinkers; the bad times are perhaps over, or explainable on a thousand and one physiological or psychological counts which could happen to anyone; they'll try again. And try they do, with and without self-imposed limitations as to times, brands, types of drinks, places, etc., etc. —courting inevitable disaster.

The progressive nature of alcoholism is one of its distinguishing characteristics. It is unfortunately impossible, in the present state of scientific knowledge on the subject, to spot alcoholics in the early years of their drinking (with notable exceptions), although there do appear, in most cases, some faint signs identifiable by an informed and careful observer, and easily identifiable by an informed and aware potential alcoholic himself.

It is this inevitable progression, along with the striking similarity of the signs and symptoms marking the progression—both of which appear in identical forms in all kinds of highly differentiated individuals—which mark alcoholism for the disease it is. Background, environment, race, sex, social status—these make no appreciable difference when once the disease takes hold of the individual. For all intents and purposes he might just as well then be labeled with a number: he has become just another victim of the disease of alcoholism.

Causes of Alcoholism

Almost everyone who has given it any thought at all, has had an opinion on "the" cause of alcoholism. These opinions, however, have differed widely. The temperance groups have held that alcohol was "the" cause, and the only cause. The "wet" groups, not only the dispensers of liquor, but many drinkers as well, have held that "the" cause lay in the individual drinker's own deliberate abuse of the privilege of drinking. A third major opinion held that alcoholism was caused entirely by the drinker's lack of will power or character.

Apart from these three general opinions, there have been a myriad of individual opinions, developed to meet individual cases of alcoholism. In one particular case "the" cause might be a wife, or mother, or husband: "He'd be all right if it wasn't for——." In another it would be a job, or the lack of one: "His job makes him drink like that," or "If he could get a decent job, he wouldn't drink so much." In still another alcoholism would be laid to bad companions: "If he'd get out of that crowd, he wouldn't drink that way." And again to geography: "He ought to go to——. He doesn't belong in this town." Or to other circumstances: "He has such problems. If he could find a solution to——, I'm sure he'd be all right." In each of these individual opinions (and there are hundreds more of a like kind) it is assumed that a particular thing or person or circumstance is the cause, and *if it could be removed, normal drinking would follow.*

Modern scientific research has not found "the" cause of alcoholism, if indeed one single cause exists. Research to date has nevertheless made a major contribution: it has swept away the above confusions by throwing its searchlight on each of them in turn, and showing that in the light they did not hold up.

In the case of the opinion that alcohol was the sole cause, scientists have pointed out that alcohol does not do the same things to all people; that the great majority of drinkers do not become alcoholics; that, therefore, it must be the man into whom the alcohol goes who is the source of the trouble. They did not then simply blame the individual alcoholic drinker and let it go at that, as both the "abuser" and "lack of will power" theories do. Instead, science began studying alcoholics, physiologically, psychologically, and as a product of their environment. In the case of the "deliberate abuse" opinion, scientists have written that an alcoholic is one "who has an *uncontrollable* craving for alcohol and uses it excessively." [3] "Uncontrollable" drinking is obviously quite different from deliberate abuse. The opinion that the drinker's weakness of will or character is "the" cause of his alcoholism is also discounted by this statement, as well as by the disease concept. These same findings destroy the

---

[3] *Alcohol Explored,* Howard W. Haggard (M.D.) and E. M. Jellinek (D.Sc.), Doubleday, Doran & Co., 1942.

over-simplified notions that any one particular external factor can be the cause of this disease, so that its removal will automatically solve the problem.

Science in fact has found many possible causes of alcoholism, so many that one scientific paper makes the statement: "It would appear that alcoholism, like fever, is symptomatic of an almost limitless variety of causes." [4] Research in alcoholism is still pitifully small and scattered, badly hampered by inadequate financing. Nevertheless it has turned up many clues, and produced some definite opinions.

These scientific opinions were at first divided into two main schools of thought: the physiological and the psychological. Some scientists and practicing physicians held the belief that alcoholism was wholly physiological in origin. Other scientists and other physicians, particularly psychiatrists, were equally certain that the origins were entirely psychological. While these two groups still have many adherents, recent years have brought other schools of thought into being. As facts have accumulated, scientific interest has mounted and spread, and theories have multiplied. Many workers in the field have come to believe that the answer will be found somewhere in the middle, with psychological, physiological and social factors uniting to create the perfect soil-bed for the monster growth of alcoholism.

Only time and more research will prove which views are correct. They have all been propounded in innumer-

---

[4] "Endocrine Treatment of Alcoholism," John W. Tintera (M.D.) and Harold W. Lovell (M.D.), *Geriatrics*, Sept.-Oct., 1949.

able scientific papers, but the evidence to support any one above the others is still lacking. The present situation has been admirably summed up in a recent publication of The American Foundation: *Medical Research— A Midcentury Survey*,[5] as follows:

It is probable that for a long time there will continue to be a division of emphasis among a number of groups, dominantly interested, respectively, in physiological, or in biochemical, or in neurophysiological, or in psychological approaches to the problem, and especially between the two large groups roughly comprising those that see alcoholism as a metabolic disease of which behavior is merely a symptom and those that see it primarily as a psychic disturbance. *The division of emphasis does not greatly matter so long as research proceeds along all these fronts, or more accurately, has in view all these approaches.*

Three of these points of view have been succinctly stated in articles appearing in the *Quarterly Journal of Studies on Alcohol*, as follows:

1. Our laboratory and clinical studies of alcoholism during the past several years have convinced us that alcoholism is a metabolic disease.—JAMES J. SMITH, M.D., *formerly Director of Research on Alcoholism, New York University-Bellevue Medical Center.*

2. The psychiatric literature of the past few years has stressed more and more the fact that compulsive

---

[5] *Medical Research—A Midcentury Survey.* Published for The American Foundation by Little, Brown & Co., 1955. Vol. 2, pp. 552-553.

drinking is a symptom and a result of personality disorder.—JAMES H. WALL, M.D., *Assistant Medical Director, the New York Hospital, Westchester Division.*

3. . . . environmental factors are potent and indispensable for bringing about alcoholism, but they do not do so unless the person involved possesses the type of metabolic individuality which predisposes toward addiction.—ROGER J. WILLIAMS, Ph.D., D.Sc., *Professor of Chemistry and Director, Biochemical Institute, University of Texas.*

In the light of these statements, it appears as much a misstatement to label alcoholism a condition caused solely by alcohol as to say that its cause is simply a lack of will power. And the current popular explanation among the half-informed—that alcoholism is "nothing but an escape"—would seem to be, at the very least, an oversimplification. None of these unscientific opinions contributes to a solution of the problem, either generally or specifically. Where they have been used as a basis for action, there has been little or no result.

Undoubtedly the solution would be very much easier if there were a single, well-defined cause of alcoholism: a microbe or a virus, for instance, or just the substance alcohol itself, or an identifiable physical deficiency. But like cancer, heart diseases and many other baffling ills, alcoholism awaits further study and research before any such enormously helpful conclusions can be made. Unlike these "popular" diseases, alcoholism has not yet received millions of dollars for research, but education has already produced drastic changes in public attitudes, and the next few years may tell a different story. The public is now demanding that science turn its full attention to this major threat to human health, and seek out the knowledge so desperately needed.

This does not mean that no solutions are possible. As in heart disease, cancer, etc., much can be done for the victims, even though it must wait until they show signs of being victims. Hope for the recovery of the alcoholic is a reality today, largely because there is —despite many conflicting opinions among scientists— general agreement that alcoholism is a medical problem of the first order. Whether the doctor or the scientist labels it a disease, an illness, a sickness, an ailment, a disorder, or merely the symptom of an underlying personality disorder, the point is that they *have* labeled it, and placed it within their province.

The *Journal of the American Medical Association* published, completed in 1957, a series of articles on alcoholism, prepared by members of the Committee on Alcoholism of the AMA's Council on Mental Health. The introduction by Richard J. Plunkett, M.D.,[6] secretary to this Committee, included the following statement:

In view of American medicine's recognition of alcoholism as a disease and not as a problem of morals . . . the Council and its Committee members believe that an intensive effort is now necessary to provide these patients with the proper medical care and consideration they so urgently need.

[6] *Journal of the American Medical Association*, December 29, 1956, Vol. 162.

2
WHAT IS AN ALCOHOLIC?

An alcoholic is a very sick person, victim of an insidious, progressive disease, which all too often ends fatally. An alcoholic can be recognized, diagnosed, and treated successfully. An alcoholic cannot be cured of his disease so that he can drink normally again. But his illness can be arrested so successfully that he can lead a perfectly normal and happy life without drinking. All of this can take place provided he is recognized as an alcoholic, and brought to recognize this fact himself. And, as in any other illness, the sooner alcoholism is recognized and treated, the better for everyone concerned.

There is no longer any valid reason why such recognition and treatment should not be possible with the vast majority of alcoholics. The identifying symptoms are known, and have been catalogued again and again in scientific, professional, and even in some popular, journals. They need only to be learned and used by those in a position to make use of them.

17

The pattern of symptoms which identifies the alcoholic is largely one of behavior, brought on by both psychological and physiological motives and reactions. There exist also both psychological and physical symptoms visible to the close observer.

The behavior symptoms are, of course, the most obvious to the layman. They are first noticeable to the immediate family or the very close friends of the sufferer, and only become obvious to the world at large when they have reached a fairly advanced stage. Largely for this reason the average person has concluded that the alcoholic is responsible for and could control such behavior. Thus alcoholism has not generally been considered a disease, but rather a matter of "bad" behavior, deliberately indulged in by the alcoholic for reasons of his own.

To the student of alcoholism, however, or to certain sensitive and understanding people who were close to some alcoholic, whether they were physicians, researchers, or merely very observant laymen, the almost unvarying pattern of these behavior symptoms has long been revealing of much more than merely a "bad" or "weak" character. Psychological symptoms, too, of which the alcoholic himself usually seemed unaware, showed themselves to the acute observer, while physical symptoms were often both visible and revealing. In short, the concept of alcoholism as a disease has been accepted by many down through the years since (and very probably long before) Dr. Rush and Dr. Trotter publicly advanced it.

It is important, however, to state and restate that for the layman, the general public, acceptance of this concept is a necessary prerequisite to any constructive action. This is true whether that action be general, for the benefit of many alcoholics, or specific, for the benefit of a particular alcoholic and, therefore, of his associates as well. It would be of very dubious value to all concerned to study the symptoms, become proficient in the identification of alcoholism, and then act as though the affliction were not only self-induced, but amenable to simple self-discipline. Such a contradiction in terms has occurred far too often, and with naturally disastrous, or at the very least unsatisfactory, consequences.

In listing the identifying symptoms it becomes possible to show clearly the progressive nature of alcoholism, for they fall naturally into three major groupings: early, middle, late or advanced. Under these broad headings a further clarifying breakdown can be made: of behavior, and of psychological and physical manifestations.

Early Symptoms

There exist perhaps many more indicative signs than those listed below. The effort here is to give enough information to be used constructively as an aid to identification of incipient alcoholism. They have been gathered largely from the recollections of recovered alcoholics, many of whom, on looking back with perspective and honesty, have stated over and over again that they now realized they had never been "normal" drinkers; that the signs had been there from the very first drinking; and that, had they known and been able to recognize those signs, they might have saved themselves years of suffering. In some cases this last has been possible; one of these will be described.

Behavior. 1. Making promises about drinking. This outstanding behavior symptom of alcoholism is only slightly apparent in the early stages of the disease. The incipient alcoholic doesn't actually make promises to anyone at this stage—he doesn't need to. He may promise himself "to do better next time" or "to be more careful in future" if his behavior causes any comment or worries him. But his public statements are generally confined to casual announcements that he "knows his limit now and intends to stick to it," or, very occasionally, that he "rather thinks he'll give up drinking for a while—next week" (or next month). Rarely does he carry out either of these half-promises. And while his drinking behavior is not yet bad enough to cause much comment on this, it usually worries the alcoholic himself a great deal, a fact which he carefully conceals, and lies about, if asked.

2. "Lying" about his drinking. The so-called lying of an alcoholic begins, in a small way, at this early stage. It is still slight enough, and about matters seemingly unimportant enough, to be overlooked, *even by himself.* Perhaps unfortunately, nearly everyone tells little social white lies on occasion, and they are pretty universally accepted, so these seem no different. In most cases such little white lies are believed by their perpetrator after one or two tellings, and the incipient alcoholic is no exception. Certainly his lies are hardly ever noticed at this stage, and would never be spotted as a symptom of anything, unless of ineptness at social finesse. Neverthe-

less, this is the start of an insidious pattern which will later be identified as the symptom called "rationalization" or "the alibi structure," pointed to by many as the dividing line between ordinary excessive drinking and the disease of alcoholism. In my opinion, this begins much earlier than is usually thought, and in such a normal everyday fashion that only the originator would or could be aware of it. But he is no more informed than anyone else. He has never been alerted so he could be on the lookout for such signs. Quite simply and naturally, as he comes to believe his little lies himself, he extends them to cover his growing "difference" from other drinkers. What most peope fail to understand is that his need is to conceal this difference *from himself*, far more than from other people, for it makes him very uneasy. It is bewildering and a little frightening. And so he minimizes the number of drinks he had at any given time, sometimes by half, sometimes by much more, depending on the extent of his fear of being "different." Occasionally he conceals the fact that he had any drinks at all ("I came straight home—didn't stop with the boys"). He may also at this stage deny that he was drunk the night before ("Of course I got a bit high—everybody did") or ("It was Joe who got drunk, so, of course, he thought I was, too. As a matter of fact, *I* got *him* home").

3. Gulping drinks ("other people drink so slowly").

4. Taking a drink *before* going to a party where there undoubtedly will be drinking, or *before* an appointment at which drinking would be quite in order.

5. Feeling the necessity of having drinks at certain regular times, *i.e., must* have a cocktail or two before

lunch, so cannot go to a restaurant which does not serve liquor; *must* have drinks at five thirty, so any meeting at that hour must be in a bar or cocktail lounge, and if no such appointment is in sight, someone must be persuaded to go.

6. Must have a certain span of time allotted for drinking before dinner regardless of any inconvenience to others, *i.e.*, in cases where late work sometimes precludes the regular visit to the bar or cocktail lounge, and even in some cases where this regular visit has already taken place, a certain (variable) amount of time for drinking must elapse before dinner can be served or ordered. Even in the early stages this may gradually come to include lunchtime also. At this point eating itself does not seem to be much affected. At times the incipient alcoholic may toy with his food after too long and too busy a pre-meal drinking interval; at other times he may wolf his lunch or dinner with a liquor-plus-delay-induced voracious hunger. Mostly he eats normally and well, if somewhat later than others might wish.

7. Must have drinks with any special event: going to the theatre, to a concert, to a baseball, football, hockey or any other game; at a meeting with an important person or persons, social or business; at a dinner or any other party; on a weekend or Sunday jaunt even to the woods or the beach "for a healthy outdoors time"; going to a wedding, a funeral, or a christening; even just having friends in to dinner or for the evening, or going to such an informal gathering.

8. Must have drinks for that tired feeling ("nothing else helps").

9. Must have drinks for nerves: because of a shattering day at the office, a frantic day with household problems, the children, or even just the state of the world. Again, "nothing else will do it."

10. Must have drinks so worry or troubles can be forgotten for a while. This one and the next are alleged to be "musts" for the sake of others, so a pleasant front can be presented, and they doubtless achieve that goal, but at the expense of dragging the incipient alcoholic nearer to disaster.

11. Must have drinks for depression ("can't see people or do anything in this state").

Psychological. 1. Most of the above come under this heading as well as under *Behavior*. They indicate a *dependence* on alcohol to do for the individual what normal drinkers and nondrinkers manage to do for themselves, sometimes with, but equally often without, the aid of drinking. This is particularly true for No. 6, where the necessity of having plenty of drinking time before dinner is usually described as being needed for relaxation from the efforts of the day before food can be enjoyed or properly digested. It is also true in Nos. 7, 8, and 9. These and other of the behavior symptoms also indicate a *compulsion* to drink rather than to see the situation through by other means. Often enough the incipient alcoholic recognizes that drinking is out of order at that particular time or place, but does not seem able to control his urge to have drinks. Often, too, he recognizes and even agrees verbally that one or two drinks should be plenty under the circumstances, but he seems driven to make it three, four, or five, regardless of his statements, and regardless of the conspicuous position it may put him in.

2. Certain other of the behavior symptoms reveal psychological symptoms even more meaningful than those showing dependence. No. 3, gulping drinks, can be interpreted as indicating a fear that the drinker will not get enough alcohol to do the jobs listed under following symptoms. This behavior symptom can also be read as a physical symptom, as will be seen later.

NOTE: Incidentally, both the dependence and the compulsive symptoms could be interpreted as physical symptoms, and are by some researchers in alcoholism. The division in scientific opinion as to the nature of alcoholism—whether it is a physiological, a psychological, or a social illness, or some combination of these—has been discussed in the chapter on causes.

3. Feelings of inferiority and inadequacy are indicated in the need for drinks listed as Nos. 4 and 5, which involve meeting other people or being in company. These are dangerous exaggerations of the normal use of drinking as a "social lubricant," and are repeated in the following symptom.

4. Feelings of isolation or "not belonging" are also indicated in the "must" factor listed under 5 and 6. The alcoholic frequently states that he cannot join in, or feel a part of a group, without drinks.

To sum up, it is the "must" or dependence on drinking which emerges as the major psychological symptom of the early stages of alcoholism. It is true that there are nonalcoholic drinkers who feel or show some of these "musts," but rarely do they feel all or even most of them.

Drinking daily at regular times is not enough to indicate incipient alcoholism, nor is the feeling that certain types of events call for drinking. Both of these last-named customs are widespread in our society. There must be shown an overwhelming majority of the symptoms listed here to qualify for incipient alcoholism.

Physical. 1. Gulping drinks is a physical symptom as well as a behavior and psychological one. Most alcoholics have a great capacity and carry their liquor unusually well during the first years of their drinking (there are, as mentioned before, certain notable exceptions). For this reason they are rarely noticeable to the uninformed (and particularly to themselves) except as lusty, "good" drinkers who can outdrink their companions with no apparent harm. They are remarkably free of "rubber legs," speech thickness, etc. even during drinking bouts. All of this actually indicates that the incipient alcoholic needs more than the normal amount of alcohol to arrive at the state of mellowness, or relaxation, or carefreeness, which is the avowed intention of all drinkers. And this extra need is indicative of his condition as an incipient alcoholic, as is his compulsion to satisfy that need regardless of circumstances.

2. Hangovers are not by any means universal among alcoholics in these earliest stages; in fact many don't have them, whereas most normal drinkers do, after an evening of overindulgence.

3. Alcoholics rarely get actively sick while drinking to excess, whereas, again, many nonalcoholics do. The nausea of the alcoholic is reserved for the next morning, but not usually until much later in his drinking career.

4. Blackouts frequently begin at this stage, although usually not till the end of a hard drinking evening. They are, of course, not visible to anyone, since the victim of the blackout is walking and talking as usual. He alone realizes the next day that events became hazy and then disappeared entirely from his consciousness at a certain point in the evening. At this stage of his illness, the alcoholic, still not realizing that his drinking is different from anyone else's, may well admit to the blackout, and ask his companions what he did, what happened, and how he got home (he usually does get home at this stage).

5. As a rule alcoholics do not often pass out in the early years of their drinking. For our purposes here we will limit the use of the term "pass out" to occasions when sleep or unconsciousness overcomes the drinker during the progress of a drinking party or bout, and not include the occasions when it may or may not have occurred after getting into bed.

In concluding this listing of many of the early symptoms, it is important to state that in alcoholism, as in every disease, there are exceptions to the general pattern. One whole group of alcoholics make the most notable exception: these are the ones who leap straight into full-fledged alcoholism at the very first drink they take, which is sometimes as early as fourteen or fifteen years of age. Perhaps because of their extreme youth, it is easier for their families and friends to accept the fact that they are ill, and to seek medical or psychiatric help for them.

Harold T. was such a case. He was first hospitalized by a frantic and bewildered family when he was seventeen. After months of treatment, first in the hospital and then as an out-patient, he was discharged by the doctors with many reservations as to whether or not he had recovered. He soon resumed drinking, but managed to space his alcoholic bouts so that he was able to work and even to achieve some success. His psychiatric treatment had helped him with many other of his problems, and also had given him enough insight into himself so that he was seriously concerned about his inability to stop drinking entirely. He sought and found further information about alcoholism, and, with help, was eventually able to cut drinking out of his life.

At the other end of the age scale is the story of Mrs. F., eighty-year-old matriarch of a large and prominent family in a famous old New England town. Never in her life had she tasted alcohol until, at a fragile seventy-nine, her doctor prescribed a little port or Madeira for her health. Almost immediately her family discovered that the bottles were disappearing, and then that she herself was disappearing into a nearby town, whence terrible tales came back to plague the family pride: of mayhem in public bars, of teetering progress down the main street with a bottle tucked under each arm, of agitated policemen confronted with a disintegrated figure they had respected since childhood. They took the only possible out, and when last heard of the old lady was enjoying herself in a good sanitarium where the kindly doctors allowed her four drinks a day, and she spent her time conniving to get five or six.

These notable exceptions make an interesting group, and there are enough of them, so that they call for special mention. It should be added that they fall into all the age groups in between the extremes mentioned above, for some immediate alcoholics took their first drink at 30 or 35, some at 28, 34, or 40, etc., etc. The important point is that these people instantly became easily identifiable alcoholics.

One other group also forms a notable exception: the periodics. Their deviation from the general pattern of alcoholism is not great *during* their drinking periods. The outstanding difference with them is the often long and apparently natural and comfortable nondrinking periods. As the disease progresses, their symptoms progress in the ordinary way, and the periods of nondrinking tend to grow shorter. In some periodic alcoholics the cycle of drinking periods becomes stabilized quite early, and remains throughout at six-month, three-, two-, or even one-month intervals. Others never have a regular cycle and can never be sure when an attack of drinking is going to hit them. On the whole, while they do constitute an exception because of their periodic nondrinking, they fall within the general pattern.

But there are individual exceptions all down the line insofar as hard and fast rules are concerned. This must be so in a disease where the main body of symptoms are to be found in behavior, since it is possible for behavior to be controlled from without as well as from within, and also since certain cultural and environmental factors can repress and delay the outbreak of certain patterns of behavior, sometimes for a very long time.

In spite of the possibilities of deviation from the general pattern, however, experience has shown that most alcoholics fall within it. The time factor, for instance, holds pretty well throughout the great body of alcoholics. Early symptoms average ten years in duration before definitely progressing to middle symptoms. There is, of course, some progression in the symptoms themselves during those first ten years, from the faint visibility of one or two up to the clearly possible identification of all of them; and from the slightly irregular happening of some of them, to the regular occurrence of them all. This lengthy period of slow progression during the incipient stage of alcoholism is the major obstacle to prevention through early diagnosis and treatment. Most alcoholics are totally unaware during this period that their drinking is any different from anyone else's; their families and friends are, as a rule, equally unaware. Again and again one can hear newly recovered alcoholics state that they were "social drinkers for the first ten years" of their drinking. One hears the same statements from families, "He drank so well for years, and then suddenly . . ." or "She never drank too much until . . ." But is this so? Accumulating evidence from recovered alcoholics themselves would seem to indicate that it may not be; that perhaps the drinking was always different from normal or social drinking, long before there were any evil consequences of that difference. In recent years, too, there have been many alcoholics in the early stages of their illness who have recognized it, have sought help, and have achieved recovery.

Peter R., for example, was a young man apparently without any major problems. In his late twenties, he was happily married with two children, and doing a job he liked and which had great potentialities. Nevertheless he sometimes worried about his drinking, and his wife Ellen was very concerned about the *way* he drank. Not that he actually got into trouble, but . . . The full gamut of early symptoms was there, and while neither Peter nor Ellen knew how to string them together, nor what significance this might have, each felt uneasy. Ellen took action. She had a college friend whose husband had recovered from serious alcoholism, and she asked questions and learned many revealing details. Finally she persuaded Peter to listen to the friend and her husband and, through them, to other recovered alcoholics. She secured literature and they both read it. It took time and the unwelcome assistance of several near-tragic drinking episodes, but Peter eventually recognized what was happening to him. More important, he clearly saw the progressive nature of those happenings, and was able to project his imagination ahead to the future probabilities if he remained in the grip of that progression. He managed to stop drinking without too much effort.

There are many more such cases that could be described. The central theme of them all is the finding of information on alcoholism: what it is and how it operates on the individual; what are the signs to watch for, and what one can do about it. Most of these cases have happy endings, first because they were able to find this information, and second because they believed not only what they could test on themselves, the symptoms and their progressive nature, but also the answer: no drinking at all. That such happy endings could occur for so many alcoholics in the early stages of their disease, even while information was so scattered and difficult to come by, is indicative of the great amount of good that should come from making such information more available.

Middle Symptoms

It will be readily seen in reading through the following listing that the middle symptoms are largely a continuation and intensification of the early symptoms. This, of course, would be expected in any other disease, but always seems to come as a surprise to people who have to cope with alcoholics, as well as to alcoholics themselves. The surprise is probably due first to the lack of acceptance of alcoholism as a disease, and second to the lack of understanding of its progressive nature. There are, however, a number of symptoms which make their first appearance at this stage of the illness.

Behavior. 1. Promises. At this middle stage the alcoholic's promises begin to come thick and fast. He promises his wife "never to do it again." He promises his boss that he "won't let it happen again." His apologies to friends and acquaintances include definite promises of better behavior next time. Particularly he promises himself: to take better care, to exercise more control, to watch his step. And he means every one of his promises. He tries desperately to keep them, failing utterly to realize that he hasn't a chance. This failure of realization isn't all his fault, or his wilful blindness. Lack of knowledge—sheer ignorance about alcoholism—must bear most of the blame. Very few alcoholics—or their families—understand what alcoholism is. This means that they often fail to recognize the alcoholic for what he is. For the alcoholic, this failure of recognition of himself *as an alcoholic* means that he cannot possibly know what to do about his drinking. Quite naturally he assumes, as others do, that he can control it, and he believes in his own promises that he will control it in the future. Unfortunately for him, everyone else believes it, too; and when he does not keep his promises they blame him for the failure. Up to now it has been the rare case who somehow intuitively recognized that no control was possible, and made his promises "never to drink again." This too, however, is an almost impossible promise for an alcoholic to keep, without outside help. But in a few scattered cases it has been done. Some alcoholics have been able to stop drinking for good, alone and unaided save by their own will and fortitude ("stubbornness" is what one of them called it). Unfortunately for the great majority of alcoholics, for whom this is impossible, these pitifully few cases have been bruited about widely enough to cause most people to think it possible for all alcoholics, which is far from true. The majority undoubtedly require expert assistance if they wish to achieve permanent sobriety. And none of them, at this stage of our knowledge, can hope to achieve controlled drinking. It is not possible even for the incipient alcoholic, if his condition is really alcoholism.

2. "Lying" about his drinking has now become an integral part of the alcoholic's life. The fact that his drinking is different from other people's is constantly showing up, with a consequent increase in his bewilder-

ment and fear. Unless he has learned something about alcoholism and its progressive symptoms (and fortunately more and more people now have this vital information), he can not understand what is happening to him—why his drinking has "changed." He is making superhuman efforts to hold it in check. His repeated failures terrify him, and make him doubt his sanity. But if he is insane, he should be locked up, he thinks (for the average man knows little of mental illness and its treatment, and fears it disproportionately), and this he can not face. So he is forced to deny the whole frightening picture, to try to explain it away, to put it in terms he *can* understand. He is fighting for his belief in his own sanity, without which he cannot function. Hence his "lies," his rationalizations, his painful construction of the "alibi structure." To attempt to destroy this structure head on, without some deep reassurance to put in its place, might well be to bring on a real mental breakdown, for this is his protection and his need for it is desperate. His need to have others respect it and leave it untouched is even greater, for it is a fragile construction at best, as he instinctively knows. His "lies" now are apt to be elaborate, constructed to minimize the amount he drinks and to explain why— on each occasion—it does such appalling things to him. For himself, he must also perpetuate the myth that he can control his drinking, or stop entirely, *if he wishes.* On this belief depends his belief in his sanity. To others he must give "logical" reasons that will deflect criticism or prevent scenes, either of which might tear holes in the sheer web of his protective structure. And, of course, he must fight with words of explanation to keep his home, or his job. This "lying" is resorted to, not by choice, but as a desperate necessity, to stave off disaster which seems to the alcoholic too great to contemplate.

3. Gulping drinks now includes taking care that he doesn't have to wait for the slow ones to catch up. At home he always fixes the drinks; if out, he offers to, with an urgent insistence. To avoid risks he carries his own supply, disappearing between servings to sample it.

4. He makes sure of having enough "under his belt" before going anywhere at all, even to a scheduled drinking party.

5. The "must" times of the day are pushed ahead: the alcoholic arrives for a lunch date fifteen minutes or a half hour early, in order to get several drinks down before the date arrives. Cocktail-time appointments are set for five or even four thirty if at all possible; he also arrives early for these.

6. He prefers to have the allotted span of drinking time before meals at a bar rather than home. This results in frequent arrivals home long after the dinner hour, often somewhat or very much the worse for wear. If the alcoholic is the wife, it means that dinner is not ready, with feeble excuses as to why it isn't; or in a case where there are servants, the wife is not ready, but remains closeted in her room, again with feeble excuses or even with none at all. Where dinner is out, the alcoholic either arrives very "high" or very late, or both; or insists on drinking time first, regardless of the time or of the lack of enthusiasm of his companion. Variations on this also hold for the lunch hour. As to the eating itself, that is growing

irregular. When he arrives home after the dinner hour he usually doesn't eat. He may toy with his plate, but if the family has waited for him, the inevitable row over his tardiness more often gives him an excuse to sulk at, or away from, the table. If his dinner has been kept for him, it's "no good" or "cold," or he's too angry to eat, because they didn't wait, or made a fuss. Sometimes he claims to have eaten before coming home. The point is that he now misses many meals, sometimes making up for it by munching at odd times; after an uneaten lunch, grabbing a sandwich in midafternoon; after a skipped dinner, raiding the icebox in the early morning hours. This last can be a Gargantuan feast, for the alcoholic, as the effect of his drinks wears off, is often afflicted with what is aptly called "the chuck-horrors," and cannot seem to get enough to satisfy his acute hunger.

7. He must be "well away" for any special event: it calls for either celebration or consolation, or it is a beastly bore and cannot be got through sober.

8. He is always "dog-tired and cannot go on without something to drink."

9. He is always "nervous" and cannot calm down enough to function without drinks.

10. He is plagued with worries and troubles: life is insupportable without drinks. This is now rarely cloaked under a supposed concern for others.

11. Depression is also a constant companion and must be dealt with by drinking.

The last four symptoms, 8, 9, 10 and 11, are of course interchangeable and appear alternately, although sometimes grouped in twos, threes, or even all together The following symptoms are new, although the germs of them can be detected in the early symptoms.

12. The accepted drinking times are now added to with increasing frequency, by a quick pickup or maybe two or three at eleven A.M. The same happens at four P.M. The alcoholic no longer cares about company, but prefers sneaking these off-hours drinks, and does not readily admit to having done so.

13. Drinking alone, which may have happened occasionally in the early stages, now increases. A bottle is kept in the desk, or hidden at home, for purely private consumption.

14. Signs of having been drinking, even of actual intoxication, begin to show at the wrong times—in the office, at sober gatherings, when people arrive, etc.

15. Weekends are apt to become real bouts, with Sundays still reserved for "straightening out," but often matching Saturday in the intensity of drinking, and causing epic Monday hangovers, with an occasional missed Monday morning at the office; or Monday "sick headache" if the alcoholic is a housewife.

16. There is at first an occasional morning drink to "get going." This is apt to increase rapidly in frequency as its efficacy becomes known and appreciated.

17. The alcoholic during this phase starts "going on the wagon" when things get a little tough due to his changing drinking behavior. He is quite able to do this for rather extended periods at this stage of his alcoholism, and this ability is apt to give him a false confidence in his power over alcohol, which too often results in even

worse behavior at the end of the period. It is worth noting here that normal social drinkers rarely feel the need to "go on the wagon," unless on very definite medical advice for some quite other ailment.

18. There is a highly noticeable irritability during periods of nondrinking, however short. The alcoholic's behavior with everyone, family, friends, business acquaintances and colleagues, labels him as a "difficult" person, overquick to anger and resentment. He is equally overquick in all emotional responses. By friends, this is usually put down to a high sensitivity, which is, of course, quite true, but it is only a part of the story.

19. Episodes of real drunkenness occur more and more often during this middle phase of alcoholism. The behavior during drunkenness also begins to change, so that the "difference in character" of the alcoholic when drunk, as opposed to when he is sober, or how he used to be, becomes more and more noticeable. People begin to mention his "Jekyll and Hyde nature." It would be futile to attempt to list these changes, for they are a highly individual matter, and depend on the particular personality of each alcoholic. The common denominator is the change itself, which is almost universal.

Psychological. 1. The growing dependence on alcohol indicated in the early symptoms has now given way almost entirely to compulsion. The alcoholic seems no longer able to function well without drinks, and apparently makes little effort to do so. The fact that he makes so little visible effort does not mean, however, that he *actually* makes no effort. It does mean that whatever efforts he makes are unavailing against his growing compulsion to drink. He is getting out of control insofar as his drinking is concerned. As the symptoms increase in intensity and frequency, the last vestiges of his control disappear. This is the major psychological symptom of the middle phase of alcoholism, and it is conspicuously progressive. It shows in all the above-listed symptoms. His changing behavior about eating, for instance, is both a psychological and a physical symptom of his growing compulsion to drink. He *must* feel the effects of that drink. If he ate normally and at normal times, the food would lessen these effects. He not only knows this instinctively, but also has proved it by experience. Therefore he puts off or avoids eating with increasing frequency. He'll "spoil the 'glow' by eating."

2. The alcoholic's attitude toward his drinking, as expressed in his conversation, is changing fast. His willingness to talk about drinking at all, especially his own, has markedly decreased and toward the end of the middle stage vanishes utterly.

3. Any admission of having been just plain drunk, which is quite usual on the part of nonalcoholic drinkers (who may even boast about it) ceases entirely. He "hasn't been feeling up to par," "had eaten something," "hadn't eaten," or "was having some shots" that temporarily ruined his drinking capacity.

4. The alcoholic does not usually admit to having hangovers: this might lead to inquiries on how much he drank last night, and he is beginning carefully to conceal the facts, since he probably started drinking the morning before.

5. The feelings of inferiority and inadequacy noted

in the early psychological symptoms are now rarely apparent except during certain stages of drunkenness. The increasing use of alcohol keeps them nearly always masked from the observer. In fact, they seem replaced by very visible signs of their opposites: arrogance and agressiveness, combining to create a grandiosity of thought and behavior which is considered typical of the alcoholic.

6. The companion feelings of isolation and "not belonging" are also increasingly well hidden from the observer by a mask of alcohol which changes them into the well-known conviviality and gregariousness of the alcoholic. Only in the so-called maudlin stages of drunkenness do the true underlying feelings show through.

Physical. 1. The gulping of drinks, while still visible, is partially superseded by the secret gulping of long swigs from a private bottle. This nearly universal practice, incidentally, accounts for the "unaccountably quick tightness" of alcoholics, observed by so many of their families and friends. In most cases their capacity has not changed or lessened; but their ability to take care of their peculiar and urgent need offstage has increased. The growing demands of this compelling need leave no room for doubt as to the onslaught of alcoholism upon the unhappy drinker. And these demands for alcohol leave no room for eating—quite literally. The fact that alcohol is a food, no matter how unbalanced or poor a food it may be, means that when the drinker has a great deal of it in him, he is actually not hungry. In fact he feels quite "full," as people do when they have dined well.

2. Hangovers have now begun to raise their ugly

heads, and for the alcoholic they are ugly indeed. The widely experienced hangover of the nonalcoholic drinker is but a pale approximation of the epic horror known to the alcoholic. His hangover is not to be endured: it includes a physical near-collapse; mental remorse; emotional self-disgust; and a terrifying self-doubt because his schemes for control once again did not work; all adding up to an attack on his nerves beyond description. Anyone who has experienced such an all-encompassing onslaught on himself for any reason whatever will find little difficulty in understanding why the alcoholic resorts to a "hair of the dog that bit him" to help him withstand the onslaught, after he learns that it will invariably do just that.

3. Nausea now becomes a frequent morning-after experience, but is still rare during drinking.

4. Blackouts are increasing, and the time of their onset grows steadily earlier. Again, these are never observable to others while in progress, except for a slight glaze in the eye which may or may not indicate that you are dealing with a zombi. But they are observable to others in retrospect when the alcoholic inadvertently gives away the fact that he is hazy or oblivious to certain happenings in which he actively took part.

5. Pass-outs now occur frequently, sometimes early in the course of an event to which the alcoholic had genuinely looked forward. He finds these intolerably embarrassing, and tries to give reasons for their happening, usually similar to his reasons for having been visibly drunk.

All of these things are seriously undermining his self-confidence. He is by now painfully aware that his drinking is all too often very different from that of his friends. The occasional relief he feels from a "good" period of drinking is inevitably shattered by a new and further slide out of control. A nameless fear begins to gnaw at his vitals, permeating everything he does even when perfectly sober. He is losing his grip and he knows it, but that very knowledge and the fear of impending catastrophe which accompanies it, prevents its acknowledgement. If he pretends it isn't so, maybe it won't happen.

And so it is often more difficult to reach alcoholics at this stage of their alcoholism than either before or after. Their minds are closed by their own fear and the intensity of their own efforts to stave off that "impending disaster." They dare not stop and listen. They dare not move, and they dare not cease moving. They are caught on the horns of a terrible dilemma.

Nevertheless there have been many cases which were brought, one way and another, to seek help at this point. The middle stage may last from two to five years, but is generally swift in its running and slides all too easily into the advanced stages. Anything that can be done to halt this rapid forward march is worth doing, not only for the alcoholic himself, but for his frightened and frantic family who, at this point, are equally aware of the march of doom.

Roy P. was a highly successful businessman at the age of thirty-nine. His position near the top of a great enterprise brought him a fat income and great prestige. He had a charming wife, who had been a successful career woman when they married, and two children. To all appearances they thoroughly enjoyed their interesting and busy life. But Roy was frightened, and Ann completely terrified by his drinking. On business trips he would sometimes be gone days past his appointed return, and those days brought a strange silence to Ann and to his office. She was hard put to it to think up excuses when the office called her for information. Occasionally they called her with a message—a plausible excuse which in no way calmed her mounting fears. Roy and Ann were sophisticated intellectuals. They discussed the situation and, as a result, Roy consulted a psychoanalyst. Months of treatment brought him great enlightenment on many sources of trouble, but to his horror his drinking did not change: control seemed as elusive as before. He seemed unable to accept the analyst's suggestion that he stop drinking, at least for a while. By now he feared for his job, for their future. Ann's nerves were approaching the breaking point; she talked of leaving him. Their social life was becoming a burden to both of them, for Roy's behavior was now wholly unpredictable. Not only were invitations falling off, but they were both reluctant to issue any, for fear Roy "might not be all right." And the children seemed remote and uncertain regarding their father, whom they had once openly adored. At this point fate stepped in. An old friend of Roy's reappeared in his life, and after an exploratory meeting, announced that he had recently recovered from severe alcoholism, and had heard that Roy, too, had a problem. Could he help? Roy asked him countless questions, and for the first time heard the concept of alcoholism as a specific disease for which there was only one answer: complete and total cessation of drinking in any form. With this knowledge and the aid of his analyst, Roy was able finally to achieve that goal.

Dennis O'M. represents almost the opposite end of the scale from Roy. A semiskilled worker in a print shop, he nevertheless earned enough to support his wife, Jennie, and their six children. When Dennis began missing his dinner entirely, more often than not, Jennie didn't worry too much, even when he arrived home very late and very drunk, sometimes very belligerent. But when his pay check was docked again and again for missing Monday mornings, and he sometimes wasn't seen from Thursday to Sunday, when he rolled in minus any pay check at all, Jennie was seriously alarmed. She began taking odd jobs to assure against periodic starvation for her brood, and she alternately cajoled and threatened Dennis, who was more than worried himself. He'd had numberless warnings from his foreman, whom he liked and respected. He knew his job hung on a slim thread, though he'd had it for fifteen years. Then the thread broke, and Dennis went on a prolonged drunk. Another job—another break —another drunk. This time Dennis was picked up and taken to the city hospital's Alcoholic Ward, battered and beaten from a barroom brawl. The doctor there had knowledge of his subject; he talked kindly to Dennis, explained to him the nature of his malady, suggested Alcoholics Anonymous. Dennis listened, first to the doctor, then to visiting members of A.A., and left the hospital vowing to try this new way of life without drink. After one or two relapses he steadied on and remained sober.

It wouldn't be a fair picture without including a

woman alcoholic, for it must be remembered that women make up one sixth of the total number of alcoholics in the United States. Outnumbered though they may be, at six to one, they often make up for that fact by the virulence of their alcoholism, and the frequently greater difficulties in both reaching and treating them. Nevertheless their chances for recovery are every bit as good as a man's, and today thousands of women have recovered, at every stage of alcoholism.

Jane D. is a good example, almost average for a woman alcoholic who is a housewife. She and her husband, Wally, started out drinking together rather heavily, but he, being a nonalcoholic, maintained the same level of drinking and of handling it over the years, while Jane did not. After the birth of their second child, Wally could no longer blink the fact that Jane's drinking was creating problems. He tried all sorts of stratagems: going on the wagon with her (at first she stuck it through, later surreptitiously broke their pacts, sometimes long before he found out); only drinking after dinner; only drinking before dinner; only drinking wines (he never could understand how Jane got so drunk on sherry—*he* couldn't take more than a glass or two of the stuff); in fact many of the "experiments" which, while we have not listed them all here, are tried in sum or in part by practically every alcoholic. Wally was frantic. He worried about what had happened to the children during the day, when he came home to find Jane in a daze, with the dinner burning, or the kitchen in a mess of unfinished preparations; he worried all day when they were having people in to dinner, or were dining out with friends.

Jane worried, too, far more acutely and constantly than Wally, but she held her peace about it. Finally she talked with her baby's doctor, who told her to limit herself to two drinks before dinner—and this she could not seem to do. Secretly she went to a brain specialist. He suggested a psychiatrist and that terrified Jane into deeper silences, and heavier drinking. Then Wally came home one night with some pamphlets about alcoholism. That angered Jane. She staged a bout so severe that for several days Wally dared not leave the house to go to work. Night after night, in sleepless torment, he carefully studied the pamphlets he had brought home for Jane. Amazed and relieved at the information he found there, he laid out a plan of action. And though his patience was often sorely tried in the months that followed, he persisted in his efforts to understand. In the end Jane turned to him for help, and together they mapped a plan for the future which included treatment for her.

Enough cases such as these could be cited to fill several books. Once again the central theme is the finding of information, both on the disease of alcoholism and means of treating it. When the alcoholic has reached this stage of his illness, however, that information usually has to be found for him: by husband or wife, by relative or friend. His growing fear and isolation from the world are apt to prevent his seeking it for himself, and left to himself he might never find it, except by unhappy accident, as Dennis did. It becomes more and more a necessity for those around the alcoholic, those who make up the world in which he lives, to arm themselves with all available information, and to learn how to use it.

Late Symptoms

The late symptoms, those of advanced alcoholism, scarcely need to be catalogued for anyone. They are distressingly obvious even to the most undiscerning. But their obviousness has not been of much help in the past; rather it has been a hindrance, and that is the great paradox of alcoholism. Here are symptoms of something terribly wrong with a fellow human being; symptoms so obvious to anyone that they should act as red flags, calling out for sympathy and help. But those very symptoms, those red flags, are of such a nature that instead they actually make enemies, create distrust, and even hate. They bring down upon the victim only contempt and punishment, thereby revealing one of the more unpleasant facets of man's inhumanity to man. For the record I will list some of these symptoms; to list them all would be to dot the i's and cross the t's *ad nauseam*.

Behavior. 1—13. Almost all of these can be lumped under one statement: the alcoholic now drinks to live and lives to drink. Unfortunately for him only the last half of that revealing phrase can be seen as behavior by the world. That he lives to drink is appallingly apparent. He gulps, he swigs, he slobbers; he is almost always in the act of trying to down liquor. Anytime, anyplace, any occasion is sufficient reason; but there no longer needs to be a reason. It is as nearly a continuous process as circumstances (financial or physical) will allow it to be. In order to keep it continuous, lying of all sorts, including to himself, is resorted to as a matter of course. He must lie in order to drink; he must drink in order to live. The same holds true of promises. This process covers symptoms 1 through 13 of the Middle Symptoms list. It particularly affects that part of symptom 6 dealing with eating. The full-fledged alcoholic's eating behavior is phenomenal: he seems to many people not to eat at all—and this is not far from the truth. He rarely wants to eat, although on the few occasions when he does he gorges like a wolf: the "chuck-horrors" are very real now. People are constantly trying to force food down him, with very little success even when he honestly tries to co-operate. "Drinking to live" has almost effaced the normal "eating to live." It has also affected the promises. The promises are still going on, albeit they have changed somewhat. They have pretty well narrowed down to one: "I'll never touch the stuff again as long as I live." But by now this is almost never possible without a great deal of help, medical and/or otherwise. Nor is it possible to make promises, or to lie, as frequently as in the middle stages: the opportunities do not arise so often since the alcoholic is usually in no state to consider stopping his drinking, or to know or care what he says. Nor can they be made so widely: there no longer are many people to whom it matters. The alcoholic's world is shrinking. Alcoholism has swept over his life like a tidal wave, blotting out most of the old landmarks. But his promises to himself go on and on, even when his utter inability to keep them makes him doubt his own sanity. The promise is now more than a behavior symptom: it is a dimming symbol of hope to the alcoholic himself. As he utters it, he believes it utterly. He must believe it or he'll die. But he shatters his own belief and he doesn't die. He just gets drunk again. And again. And again.

14. Drunken behavior now usually, almost inevitably, takes place at the wrong time. On the job, in the office in the early morning following an all-night drinking bout, at an important interview for a new job (the old one having been lost for such behavior), at an important dinner or meeting, at a wedding (it has even happened to an alcoholic at his own wedding, and frequently at his son's or daughter's), or at church. By now it has happened so often at gatherings at home that he either no longer has a home, or lives there in "protected" isolation with a lost and terrified family.

To this symptom, for many alcoholics, there is often a remarkable addition. Large numbers of them have been able, while actually sodden with drink, to appear at work, at parties or other meetings, and give the impression that they are quite sober. There is a physical sign, however, known only to initiates and experts: a peculiar smell which is not exactly that of a "liquor breath" but rather an entire body aroma, not precisely of liquor, but faintly reminiscent of it, and also sweetish-sour. Once this smell has been identified, it becomes unmistakable, and it will spot an alcoholic where there is no other, or prior, knowledge of his condition. This should properly be listed under physical symptoms, but since it usually appears in conjunction with the above-named apparently sober behavior it seemed of more practical use to mention them together.

15. Drinking bouts now occur regardless of the time of week, month or year. Their duration at the intense

level varies according to the financial and physical condition of the alcoholic, from a few days to a week or longer.

16. Morning drinks are a regular necessity in order to function at all. This belongs also under physical symptoms and will be dealt with more fully under that heading.

17. Periods of "being on the wagon" still occur, but less often unless there is frequent medical treatment or hospitalization. In that case, there are sometimes quite long "dry" periods following treatment. The alcoholic very often honestly believes he is "on the wagon for keeps," and is more surprised and upset than anyone else when he falls off. In some cases he has been "obliged" to drink after a period of self-imposed and untreated abstinence because his nervous system or his physical condition did not permit him to function without drinks; *i.e.*, he could not eat, he could not shave (or use make-up), or write or do anything that requires even a moderately steady hand, because of his continual tremor. Such falls from grace appear to be deliberate behavior, but this is seldom so, even when the alcoholic, *after* the act, proclaims it to be. If he proclaims his intention before taking a drink, he will usually attempt to explain his apparently mad behavior to himself and others by saying he "can't stand it any more" or he'll "really go out of his mind if he doesn't drink" or he "can't live without it," and this is actually how he feels. This behavior is both a psychological and physical compulsion, way beyond the average alcoholic's control.

18. Irritability and high-pitched emotional responses

are now fairly constant whether actually drinking or not. In other words, the alcoholic's total behavior is extremely emotional.

19. Complete drunkenness is the alcoholic's condition most of the time, although as mentioned before it does not always show clearly. During his occasional periods of sobriety or near-sobriety, vestiges of his old or real self appear, giving rise once more to observations on his Jekyll and Hyde personality. By now, however, such observations are mostly confined to the few people who "still love him in spite of everything" (and there are a few in nearly every alcoholic's life), or to new acquaintances who still know him scarcely at all (and won't for long).

20. The alcoholic's behavior regarding jobs is one of the things that gives credence to a prevailing belief that all alcoholics are more or less insane. Although he may have been fired from a number of jobs, and any job may be getting hard to come by, he will often walk out on one with a high-flown excuse for his action. Or he will leave his desk or place "for a minute," start drinking, and never go back even to collect money owing him. There are some cases where the full-fledged alcoholic is still in the same job, or with the same firm he was with in his incipient stage. In these cases he is either being protected by his colleagues and immediate superiors because of their personal liking and sympathy for him (or sometimes for his family), and/or his work is so good in his sober intervals that he is considered worth giving an almost endless series of "one more chance." Even in

these last cases, however, the day eventually comes when they join the less fortunate ones on the merry-go-round of changing and diminishing jobs, which at the very end reaches the vanishing point of no jobs at all.

21. This in turn produces another extremely unpleasant symptom: getting money to drink, by any means possible. Ordinary borrowing, as practiced among sane and sober people, soon deteriorates (since it cannot be repaid) into "the touch." Where the home is still intact, the wife's pocketbook, or the husband's pockets, are rifled in the night, or various movable objects are sold or pawned. There is the famous—and true—story of the husband who sold the refrigerator while his wife was out buying food to put in it. Money now seems to hold no meaning for the alcoholic except in terms of how much liquor it will buy. And he acts as if he thought it rightly belonged to him because of his great need, no matter who had it before he took it. There have been many instances of alcoholics who usually were the gentlest of souls, even when drunk, suddenly resorting to violence in order to get liquor or the money for liquor. A measure of the depth and intensity of his desperate need can be taken from the alcoholic's behavior about money, for he is often fundamentally a meticulously honest person.

22. The alcoholic's behavior toward his family is another thing giving credence to many prevailing unpleasant beliefs about him. He watches them sink into destitution, or struggle out of it in spite of the burden he imposes, or leave him completely, all with apparent indifference—or at least without changing his ways. He

rarely shows his real feelings about all this to anyone, except for occasional maudlin scenes in the company of strangers, in bars.

23. If he is a Catholic, his behavior toward his priest and his Church is usually one of increasing avoidance. If he is a Protestant he probably gave up all church-going long before this stage, together with any contact with his minister, and by now is a voluble agnostic or out-and-out atheist.

24. His behavior about time shows an almost complete loss of time-sense. He rarely knows what time it is, often does not know what day it is—and to him it does not seem to matter. The world and its conventions and laws are slipping away from him fast.

To sum up, the alcoholic's resemblance to the man he was, or the woman she was, is vanishing. A few years of this completely uncontrolled kind of drinking, and the behavior it inevitably produces, and there will be a different person presented to an unsympathetic, uncomprehending world, a world which often says, "So *that's* the kind of person so-and-so really is." It is not so-and-so per se; it's *the alcoholic* in general who is like this. The many persons judged by the behavior symptoms noted above are highly individualistic *as persons*. Their true personalities are as different from one another as their fingerprints. But their behavior as alcoholics is as like as so many ball bearings. And the world judges people, first of all, by their behavior. Too few people look, or are equipped to look, for the psychological or physical reasons behind that behavior. These are symptoms, too, and they exist in other illnesses as well as in alcoholism. In the case of alcoholism particularly they often overlap and sometimes are as obvious as the behavior symptoms, especially to those with the wish to comprehend. A little clear knowledge should make it comparatively easy for anyone to recognize and understand the involuntary and helpless condition of the alcoholic; and therefore to help him to help himself.

Psychological. 1. An overwhelming compulsion is now the major psychological symptom. This is the full-fledged compulsive drinker in every sense of the word. Compulsion is the alcoholic's constant companion, whether he is actually drinking or not, for even when he is not drinking, his life is built around the bottle. This is what lies behind the unattractive, even repellent behavior which is so obvious. There is no such thing as control, even when the alcoholic seems to have temporarily regained it.

2. He no longer has any visible attitude toward his own drinking. He seems indifferent; a life of drinking is apparently completely accepted as natural and inevitable for him. With this acceptance, however, is an increased sense of shame, and deep feelings of degradation, which are at least partially responsible for his assumed indifference. There are cases where this indifference, once assumed, has become real: it is a kind of numbness, which has deadened any feelings which once hurt.

3. Admissions—of drinking or of drunken behavior—simply don't enter this picture. No discussion is willingly entered into. There are, however, rare outbursts (usually when half-drunk) of horror, self-disgust, and a tragically real desire to "be like other people."

4. The ordinary morning hangover is not allowed to occur: round-the-clock drinking prevents it. Occasional two- or three-day collapses are not conceded to be hangovers: they are some extraordinary sickness, or an extreme fatigue or inertia due to any one of a number of supposed physical ills. The night "horrors" which plague the alcoholic at this stage are never admitted as such, but are sometimes referred to as nightmares. The alcoholic himself actually is not quite sure whether they have occurred waking or sleeping; and sometimes fears they may have happened in reality. This is one of the worst symptoms, to him, and keeps him in a sweat of terror which cannot be described.

5. His feelings of inferiority and inadequacy are now frequently visible in an extreme form, contrasting sharply with equally extreme swings to grandiosity.

6. Isolation and the feeling of not belonging have become very pronounced. The alcoholic seeks only the company of others like himself, if he can find them (and he usually can). Most women at this stage avoid all company, and retire into a shell.

7. Even at this stage there are occasional times when the alcoholic manages his drinking very well. If he has a few days of enforced nondrinking, he gains a real sobriety, and on starting to drink again he sometimes achieves a normal slow progression to the state of well-being he is seeking, which stops well short of drunkenness. This may continue for several days, giving him enormous relief, but also fooling him into renewed hope that he will now be able to manage drinking "like other people." He has forgotten that other people do not

require alcohol to achieve a state of well-being. Such a state of affairs is incomprehensible to him now, and he frankly doesn't believe it. This view, incidentally, presents one of the major hazards to recovery, for it is exceedingly difficult to overcome. The alcoholic simply will not be convinced that he will ever be able to feel well and to enjoy life without drinks. It has been his sole means to both ends for too long, and his few times without drinking have never included either a sense of well-being or real enjoyment. They have, for him, been either a constant fight against his compulsion, or a static period of unhappy numbness. To convince him that there is a possibility of a bearable, even of an enjoyable life, without drinking, becomes the first task of anyone trying to help him.

Physical. 1. It is no longer a question of merely gulping more drinks than other people, either publicly or privately. There is now a pressing physical need to get and keep a certain amount of alcohol in the system at all times. This holds regardless of what form the alcohol may be in: whatever may be left in the liquor closet, including an unholy mixture of tag ends of different bottles; what is left in other people's unfinished glasses from the night before; cooking sherry or brandy; the cheapest of gins or applejacks; Listerine, vanilla, rubbing alcohol, hair tonics, perfumes; and further down the scale "smoke," canned heat, antifreeze—anything, in fact, which contains the precious, desperately needed alcohol. This physical need for a certain amount of alcohol continually circulating in the system effectively precludes eating, for food might disturb the hard-won balance, might blot out the alcohol. And again, the constant presence of alcohol eliminates hunger, so no need for food is felt, except on rare occasions.

2. Hangovers, as already explained, are not now the usual morning-after discomfort known to nonalcoholic drinkers. They do make themselves felt, however, in the peculiarly horrible form known to alcoholics, on every awakening from sleep, and wherever possible are imme- liately wiped out by drinks. Since these awakenings may ake place at any hour of the day or night, such drink- ng cannot be called strictly morning drinking, although to the alcoholic it is "as-if" morning. To him, drinks at such times are an absolute physical necessity. He literally and honestly cannot function physically without their help. For instance, he can hardly lift his head from the horizontal (the result without drinks is extreme dizziness, violent nausea, swimming vision, shuddering shakes, and sometimes a cacophony of sounds with a flashing of lights and colors); he cannot stand upright because his legs are too weak to hold him; he cannot, even leaning on some- thing, wash his face or brush his teeth because his hands are too shaky to hold anything, and furthermore are out of control, afflicted with jerks. Knowing all this, he must drink.

3. Nausea, however, is now an added problem. The drinks he must have on waking too often refuse to stay down. Some alcoholics simply accept the terrible loss of several precious drinks and persist until one does stay. Others use various techniques: pepper on the drink, sip- ping it slowly through a straw (to get tiny quantities at long intervals), putting it in milk (the home version of

the milk punch), etc., etc. Nausea at this stage is not limited to waking-up times; it may attack the alcoholic at any time or place. It also frequently prevents eating, even when earnestly attempted.

4. Blackouts set in, and disappear, at any time, leaving unaccountable memory blanks in odd sections of the day or night. They may, and sometimes do, last for several days at a stretch.

5. Pass-outs, too, happen at any old time. Since much of the alcoholic's sleep is now actually passing out, it rarely lasts long at any one time. He is inclined to sleep for an hour or two and then wake to an awareness of all the terrifying physical and psychological symptoms already mentioned. And if there is no alcohol to be found in the house or in his room at such a time, he manages by a superhuman effort of will to get himself out to look for some. It is on such occasions that he will go to any length to get the money to buy what he must have.

All of this adds up to the statement made at the beginning of this section. The alcoholic now drinks to live just as much as he lives to drink. He has arrived at a point where he literally cannot function as a human being without the aid of drinks. He has also arrived at a point where, in most cases, he loathes his bondage, despises himself for being unable to break it, but feels he must conceal these feelings since he is both helpless and hopeless. This of course applies to women as well as men. The emphasis, in describing details of certain symptoms, seems to be on how they affect men, but they can all be turned to fit the circumstances of a woman's life, either at home or in a career. While the behavior of women, especially those who still have a home, is on the whole slightly different from that of men, most of these differences are due to circumstances, and would be un-noticeable if the circumstances were the same.

The apparent hopelessness of advanced alcoholism belies the facts. In the early years of Alcoholics Anonymous, for instance, all of its successful members had first reached this point. It was in fact believed that no one could be helped until they had arrived at this advanced stage. While those opinions have had to be revised in the light of later events, it remains true that alcoholics in the full grip of advanced alcoholism can and do make dramatic recoveries.

Jack K. was such a case. He had been a railroad man all of his working life (which had begun when he was fourteen). Supremely happy in his work, he had also had a good marriage. But as his alcoholism progressed, it first disturbed and then broke up his marriage, and finally canceled out his twenty-five-year connection with the railroad. There followed a period of spotty odd jobs, with his sisters and brothers taking him in or tiding him over the bare spots. Finally they could take it no longer, and gave him the fare to a far-off city. Naturally he drank up the money and then reappeared on their doorstep. Next time they bought the ticket and gave it to the bus driver themselves. Jack alternately washed dishes and drank for the next two years, gradually arriving at the point where he could not get even the lowest, most menial paid job, or, if he got it, could not hold it through one day. Through the kindness of an overworked janitor, he slept behind the furnace in a tenement house, in return for stoking the furnace. The janitor also allowed Jack to collect the trash of the several buildings he serviced, and sell such of it as was salable for the ready cash he needed to drink. Magazines, when there were any, brought the best return, so he handled them carefully. On a clear spring day, many years ago now, his bloodshot eyes saw the words "Alcoholics Anonymous" on the cover of a tattered copy of the *Saturday Evening Post*. He put it aside, for at the moment he was in no condition to read: he had had no money for liquor for several days, and was weak, sick and shaky, totally unable to concentrate on a printed page. When he got his bottle of "smoke," he read avidly, then borrowed from his friend the janitor a piece of paper, an envelope and a stamp. His letter to A.A. brought him a visitor within a few days, and, amazed and scarce believing, Jack listened to what he was told. That was the beginning of recovery for him.

Dr. Gerald B. came from another world than Jack, but he ended living in the same one. As a young medical student he had wondered about his drinking, had read everything he found that seemed to shed light. It wasn't much. Then he began his practice and married—and seemed to "settle down." His marriage was such a remarkably happy one that it had the effect of deflecting the path of his alcoholism for a considerable time. He was wholly absorbed in his wife, in their home and children, and in his busy doctor's career. Even so the way he drank, when he did, still secretly worried him, and he vainly scanned the medical journals of several countries (for he had done his postgraduate work abroad) for information. Then, after a fifteen-year near-standstill, his symptoms began to progress, more and more rapidly. His wife managed to cover up for him, to nurse him quickly back to health after bad bouts, and he was able to approach an advanced stage of alcoholism without serious outside damage. Meanwhile their children had married and left home—and then his wife died. Everything fell apart at once. He fled to Europe, seeking information and help, and returned broke and hopeless, and sodden with drink. Now his descent was incredibly rapid. In a few months he had joined the "jungle drinkers," the lost souls who live under bridges and wander the streets in rags begging for pennies to buy their drink. Although he was in his late fifties, he managed to survive six years of that life before a lucky accident brough him in contact with a social worker who gave him the basic information about alcoholism he had so long sought in vain. His medically trained mind grasped its significance at once, and he quickly sought aid in regaining his health so that he might be able to put these new-learned facts to good use. The Salvation Army gave him shelter and food; later they used his services as a doctor, thus helping him win back his self-confidence. In time he was once more practicing medicine with special emphasis on alcoholism. He and others like him—for there are now many doctors who have recovered from alcoholism—have much to contribute to a groping world on this subject in which their knowledge is so thorough and well-rounded.

Marjorie F. came from still another world: the social world of wealth and luxury. Her mother was a leader in that world, and Marjorie was sent to fashionable schools to be prepared for a fashionable marriage. Drinking, even regularly excessive drinking, was a common-place in Marjorie's debutante and post-debutante circles, so that her own was in no way noticeable. In due course she made a socially satisfactory marriage; it did not, however, prove satisfactory to her. While it lasted, her drinking progressed more quickly than usual from the early to the middle stage of alcoholism. On its breakup she progressed equally quickly to an advanced stage. Her mother cried "nervous breakdown" and popped her into one sanitarium after another, with apparently small results. Marjorie, however, was learning. She'd had too many doctors tell her she could never safely drink again not to be half convinced, even though she did not find their explanations satisfactory. Her own experiments were lending weight to their warnings, for Marjorie was an intelligent girl, who did not like suffering, and she suffered terribly from the aftermaths of her drinking. In her round of institutions she had met one doctor in whom she had unusual confidence. She decided to put herself in his hands, remaining in his institution for nearly two years, then took a house in a nearby town for another three years. Drastic? Perhaps, but the results were worth it to Marjorie, for she hasn't had a drink since, and has been happily married and living in the West for many years now. Information and proper treatment saved her life and sanity and made happiness possible. It could do the same for thousands of others, *if it were available*.

In all the cases cited here information about alcoholism has been the key to recovery. In some very early cases, that alone has been sufficient, but in most cases it has had to be followed by some kind of outside aid.

What kind of aid is best for which cases, is a matter not so easily arrived at. Many alcoholics have tried many methods before arriving at the right one for them. And who is to say that they were not all like Marjorie, who learned a little from each try? The note of hope sounds in the fact that there is in all probability a right method for each of the several million sufferers from alcoholism if it could be found and applied to, and by, them.

3

WHO IS AN ALCOHOLIC?

It can be anyone. By this I mean that it can be a
person from any walk of life. Given the initial premise
that alcoholism is a disease, it should be easy to recognize
that it is no respecter of persons. All manner of people
fall victim to alcoholism: rich and poor, educated and il-
literate, godly and ungodly, young and old, men and
women, "good" people and "bad," charming people and
those without attraction, and everything in between.

This fact seems to come as an unending surprise.
One hears constantly such statements as: "He can't be an
alcoholic. Look at the money he makes—or the position
he holds" or: "She simply isn't the type—well brought
up, very well off, a fine marriage, three children—it just
isn't possible" or: "It must be something else—he's too
intelligent to throw everything away just for the sake of
drinking." Or even: "I don't believe he's an alcoholic.
He's a fine man, and good at his work. If such-and-such
would just happen, I'm sure he'd steady on." And again:
"It simply can't be that—why, he has everything!" Or at

the other extreme: "What else has he got? Naturally he drinks." Or: "He's just a bad lot and his drinking proves it," or: "He may have a good side, but he's a pretty nasty piece of work, and the way he drinks shows it."

All such statements stem from the outdated and faulty beliefs which have been consciously or unconsciously held by almost everyone for so long. In particular they stem from the belief that only bums, or no-goods, are drunks. The very term "alcoholic," which connotes something other than "just a plain drunk," is beginning to undermine this last notion. But it dies hard, and people find it difficult to accept the fact that their country-club friend, or their bridge partner, or the banker's wife, can be an alcoholic. Even harder to accept is the fact that doctors, nurses, priests and ministers of the Gospel can also be alcoholics, just as the butcher or the factory worker or the dockhand or any of their wives can be. It is human beings who are afflicted, not groups, classes or types.

Jane L., for instance, belonged to the leading family in a little Southern town. They had been great plantation owners since Revolutionary times, and their fortune had grown through textile mills. She was a carefully hidden family problem for years until an understanding doctor in one of the many sanitariums she had visited started her on the road to final recovery.

Sarah F. was the daughter of a worker in one of the L. family's mills. Her drinking career had been far more public and unpleasant than Jane's, and her one period of formal treatment had been when the courts intervened and committed her to the state mental institution. Jane was able to be of great help to Sarah, and they became good friends despite their different backgrounds. Sharing this common ailment brought them closer to each other than to many friends in their own respective circles.

A similar story could be told of James T., a college professor and scholar of renown, whose drinking behavior finally put him in the ranks of the unemployed. During a sojourn in an institution where alcoholism received special attention he met a truck driver from his own town, who had been sent there by a friendly and enlightened employer. They had been equally baffled by their dilemmas, and now they were drawn together by the similarity of their problems. When they went home, they maintained close contact for many years, apparently drawing strength from each other.

Alcoholics generally have more in common with each other than just their alcoholism. It has been noted time and again that alcoholism all too frequently strikes the "most promising" member of a family, a school class, or a business. Granted that it also can strike the dull, the mediocre and the misfit, nevertheless the alcoholic very often seems to be a little more alert, a little better at his job, a little more intelligent than his fellows in their particular social, economic or job level. This may well be the result of an unusual sensitivity, also widely noted by students and researchers, a sensitivity similar to that attributed to creative people. Sometimes, in fact, it would appear to be one and the same thing, as in two outstanding examples: John Barrymore and F. Scott Fitzgerald. These talented men suffered visibly and painfully, before the eyes of the whole world, from alcoholism. Tragically for them, they lived and died just a little too soon, before the world which watched their antics was able to understand why they behaved so, and to help them. The sensitivity noted in alcoholics is for them anything but a healthy or constructive thing, even when it produces the superb acting of a Barrymore, or the fine writing of a Fitzgerald. Rather than widening their horizons, and increasing their creative output, as sensitivity might be expected to do in totally healthy persons, it narrows and limits the horizons of alcoholics, by turning them in upon themselves, and away from a world which they feel does not understand them.

How can the world learn to understand them, and therefore to help them? It must first learn to recognize them, as, inescapably, what they are: victims of a disease, who can be helped and are very much worth helping. But the world can still ask: "How are we to tell? Who are these people? Which are alcoholic drinkers, which just heavy drinkers? The pattern of symptoms is revealing, very, but is there no simple definition which clearly divides the alcoholic from all other drinkers?"

There is a simple practical definition that has been frequently used to help nonalcoholics recognize the illness in someone else. Its greatest success, however, has been in helping alcoholics to recognize their own illness. Here it is:

An alcoholic is someone whose drinking causes a continuing problem in any department of his life.

The key word is "continuing," and the definition could be made still more accurate by adding "and growing," for the alcoholic's problem rarely continues for long at the same level. Only slightly less important are the words "in *any* department of his life." There must be no mistaking the meaning of this definition if it is to be of any use.

The first department of an alcoholic's life which is affected by his drinking is his inner life. He may worry slightly at one or two transgressions from acceptable drinking behavior, but when he notices that he has more such lapses than his friends—that his, in short, are continuing rather than spasmodic—he usually is very disturbed. However much he may explain this away to himself (rationalize it), or brush it aside as of no consequence, it remains a nagging doubt. And each time something he did not plan or expect occurs in connection with his drinking, the doubt rushes back to nag him. He has a continuing problem within his own mind, and deep in his heart he knows it. This may be completely hidden from any outside observer, although one who really loves him may realize even at this early point that he "has something on his mind" or is "worrying about something." Should they tax him with it, however, or suggest that it has anything to do with his drinking, they are likely to meet only violent denials, and to set up a barrier to any later discussions. It is unwise to intrude directly at this point, though indirect approaches can sometimes be made, which may bring results later.

The signs of a continuing problem usually appear next in the home life. Unusual behavior connected with drinking naturally shows up first to those closest to the alcoholic, whether they be wife, husband, mother or father, sister or brother, or roommate. And since this behavior, being out of the ordinary and therefore unexpected, is at the very least inconvenient to others, it creates a problem. Here again the direct approach is usually futile. For one thing, it is likely to be made on each occasion as a separate thing, so that there is a steady succession of small rows, followed either by increasing distance and coolness, or by increasingly fervid promises. Rarely does the nonalcoholic in the case wait to see a pattern develop and then try to work out an approach which will not drive the alcoholic into sullen silence or frenzied anger.

The social life is probably the next department to be affected. Here the peculiar drinking behavior may be accepted for quite a while, each time being forgiven as an exception, but when it becomes known as recurrent and continuing it becomes a problem, and firm action is likely to be taken: the alcoholic is simply not invited, and finds that his invitations are not accepted. He begins to change friends, moving from group to group, and this process is accelerated if any of his real friends try to "talk seriously to him about his drinking." As usual, the direct approach by the uninformed produces an effect opposite to that intended: friendships are apt to be rudely terminated, and even the subject of drinking is now a continuing problem in the social life of the alcoholic.

The time at which drinking causes a problem in the physical life of the alcoholic varies greatly in each case. But the problem is the same: a growing physical need for drinks, and the consequent inability to go anywhere or do anything without them. The disruption or intense difficulties caused by hangovers are a part of this continuing problem, too, as is frequent inability or unwillingness to eat.

Drinking may cause a continuing problem in the business or professional life of an alcoholic for a long time before any action is taken—and then, all too frequently, such action is sudden and final. If it were recognized that as soon as a man's drinking *began* causing a problem in his work he should be dealt with and treated as a sick man in need of help, and somehow brought to seek that help, many jobs and much money could be saved.

Naturally, if drinking is causing a continuing problem in all or even some of the above-named departments of life, then the financial department is going to be affected. Drinking may, in fact, cause serious problems in the alcoholic's financial affairs very early in the game, at the same time that it is causing a problem in the innermost life.

The reasoning behind this definition for alcoholism is as simple as the definition itself: if drinking is causing a continuing problem in any department of a normal or social drinker's life, he will either cut down or cut out the drinking. That is the logical or normal solution to the problem, and for a normal drinker would present no great difficulty, even though he might intensely dislike or resent having to do it. But if the drinker is an alcoholic, he may equally well realize that that is the solution; he may even say so, and be convinced that he is going to do it; but he won't do it, because he won't be able to do it. In this lies his alcoholism; and his continued drinking, for whatever reasons he may give, proves it, since it thus continues causing a problem.

It is important to realize that any one of these situations alone is sufficient reason to consider alcoholism an immediate danger to the drinker. There are undoubtedly many cases where the first noticeable sign is in the inner life. The drinker broods and worries and makes elaborate plans to avoid any untoward occurrences from his drinking. He may even discuss these plans and make bold statements as to what he is going to do. Illumination comes to the onlooker when it is observed that these plans are rarely if ever carried out: something extraordinary always comes up to upset them.

There are other cases where the first visible sign is financial. Here again, if the normal drinker finds that liquor is costing him too large a proportion of his income, he will cut down the consumption, even though he may grouse and complain bitterly about it. The alcoholic will cut down on something else, in order to leave undisturbed the amount he wants for drink. He will in fact take great care to pay his bar bills or the liquor store account first, though doing so may mean that he cannot pay the grocer or that the rent may have to wait: he does not dare let his credit lapse for this, to him, essential supply. Often this is done for a very long time, without anyone realizing its significance, and only when it is glaringly apparent that money for rent, food, clothing and everything else is secondary to money for liquor, are the observers aware that here is an alcoholic.

In attempting to make a diagnosis according to this definition, time is very important. No problem can be judged to be a continuing one until considerable time has passed. And nothing could be more dangerous to the possibilities of future recovery than a premature jumping to conclusions by an observer, with resulting premature action. It is unlikely that anyone could safely label another person an alcoholic according to this definition, unless they were very close to him, and in a position to observe the details of his daily life, or unless he were in the late stages of alcoholism.

There are other difficulties, too, in making an amateur diagnosis of alcoholism. For instance, two particular groups of drinkers exist who apparently fit the above diagnosis, but who are not regarded as true alcoholics. These are the situational drinkers, and the mentally ill drinkers. Situational drinkers may sometimes be identified as such by a well-informed but otherwise untrained observer, although it requires the utmost care and thought. But the mentally ill drinker is often exceedingly difficult to diagnose, even for the most highly trained psychiatric diagnosticians.

The situational drinker may be defined as the person who, as the result of a particular situation which he finds temporarily impossible to bear, embarks upon a period of uncontrolled, apparently alcoholic drinking. Such situations can be created by the death of someone dearly beloved, or an unintentional act which has resulted in dreadful consequences, or an irreplaceable loss of some sort which has deep emotional meaning for the individual; even by an intolerable job or home situation which circumstances prevent the individual from changing. They can also be brought about by an accident or an

illness. The situation results in drinking which has all
the earmarks of alcoholism, and in some cases it may
continue long enough to have to be treated as alcoholism,
with recovery dependent on a permanent cessation of all
drinking. In many cases, however, the period comes to an
end, sometimes naturally, more often with the aid of outside forces. Psychiatric treatment has been the most successful aid, although religion, a new love or other strong
emotional interest, or even the efforts of loyal and
understanding friends have sometimes helped. When this
happens the situational drinker is able, unlike the true
alcoholic, to resume normal controlled drinking.

Philip F. was a hard drinker from the time he began,
but that was not unusual in the circles in which he was
brought up. He was deeply devoted to his mother, whose
mainstay he had been during her difficult struggle, as a
nearly penniless widow, to bring up her family. At
thirty-two he made an unsuitable and extremely unhappy
marriage, which quickly terminated in an acrimonious
divorce. Meanwhile his mother had developed cancer,
and, shaken by his marital experience, he next had to
watch a slow and painful death. His drinking immediately went wildly out of control, and for four years
he rode the merry-go-round of alcoholic drinking. He
moved far from his own city, and went rapidly from
job to job, sliding down the economic scale each time he
moved. He made friends easily, and some of these friends
tried to help him. They persuaded him to see a psychiatrist, and to undergo treatment. After some months he
announced that on a certain date he was going to stop
drinking—and he did. For eight years he never touched

alcohol. Meanwhile he married again, very happily, rose to the top in his business, and seemed to thoroughly enjoy his life. With no reasons given, no excuses made, he started, in that eighth year, to drink beer. A year later it was observed that he occasionally took a cocktail or a highball. His drinking to date (five years later) has caused no problem, and has apparently been much more moderate than when he first drank in his youth. It seems obvious that Philip was really a situational drinker.

There is no doubt that most alcoholics would like to think of themselves as situational drinkers, because almost without exception they would like to believe that one day they could drink normally again. And indeed, most alcoholics can give a dozen reasons "why they began to drink too much" that might fool an unwary observer into believing they were in fact only situational drinkers. For these reasons it is dangerous to assume that someone whose drinking is causing you concern is merely a situational drinker and will be all right in time. Where there is really such a possibility, the safest thing is to get professional advice or, failing that, to act upon the assumption that the drinker is a true alcoholic. Incidentally few truly situational drinkers have ever shown any of the early symptoms. They usually start with the middle symptoms and rarely get further than this stage of alcoholic drinking; if they pass into the late stage, it can be safely assumed that they are true alcoholics. Also, few situational drinkers whose histories are known have attempted to move from their period of uncontrolled drinking straight to moderate drinking: there has always been an interim of no drinking at all. Most of these cases have required psychiatric treatment to help them achieve this. And, of course, there have been many cases where a true alcoholic, convinced that his alcoholism was merely a situational episode, has attempted to return to controlled drinking after a period, sometimes quite long, of abstinence. Inevitably he found himself right back in the full throes of alcoholism in very short order.

In my own opinion, there are not a great many of these situational drinkers. Occasional histories, which cover sufficient time to mean anything, do reveal them. But many other histories, when investigated after a lapse of several years, reveal that the supposed situational drinker had not been able to continue controlled drinking for very long, and had either ceased drinking entirely or slid back into active alcoholism.

Mentally ill drinkers present a real and tragic problem. In their case, too, the outward appearance is one of true alcoholism, and indeed they are alcoholics. However, their alcoholism is only a minor part of their trouble, no matter how serious it may be in itself. The problem, and the tragedy, lies in the fact that even if their alcoholism can be arrested, they are not much better off, for they are still left with their major illness which cannot always be cured. In some cases they even appear to be worse off, as if the drinking bouts had been a valve letting off dangerous steam, so that when this valve is closed there is an inevitable blowup which can be disastrous.

Karl J. was such a case. He had apparently been an immediate alcoholic when he started drinking at fourteen, and had a long history of serious trouble connected with drinking, including many jail sentences. In his thirtieth year he came into the hands of a therapist specializing in alcoholism, who believed he could help Karl, and took infinite pains, to which Karl gratefully responded. In his particular field the therapist succeeded, for Karl achieved sobriety and held it for six years, during which time he worked steadily, married, and to all appearances became a model citizen. Then the blowup came. It took the form of an outbreak of violence which brought death and disaster in its wake. Perhaps fortunately for him, Karl turned the gun on himself and closed the story.

In other cases, successfully arresting the alcoholism has had a good effect eventually, even though at first it seemed to make things worse. In these cases, alcoholism had served as a cloak, hiding the real trouble from view, and when the cloak was removed the mental illness slowly but surely revealed itself.

Beatrice K. came under this heading. She, and her family, and numerous doctors in whose care she had been placed from time to time, believed that she was an alcoholic. So she was, but . . . After many abortive efforts she finally managed to stop drinking, at a time when she was not under any particular doctor's care. The first six months were a period of intense happiness for all concerned, and then peculiar things began to happen. Family friends began to inquire about strange telephone conversations; strangers called complaining about visits and calls which they considered prying into their affairs. Certain family affairs were summarily and arbitrarily dealt with, without consulting anyone. Talking to Beatrice about these things invoked stormy sessions of alternate weeping and raging. She began staying up all night, pacing the floor and moaning or muttering to herself. She had spells of violent shuddering and crying. At last the family took her to a sanitarium, where she was diagnosed as having a serious mental illness. In her case, it had been caught much earlier than usual, and after several years of treatment, Beatrice was able to return to the normal world.

Perhaps the most tragic of the mentally ill drinkers are the so-called psychopathic personalities. Some of these people are so utterly irresponsible and so low in intelligence that it is obvious there is little help for them. Others, however, appear charming and intelligent—during their good periods. It is then easy to suppose that their strange reactions—and lack of reactions—are due entirely to their alcoholic drinking. But this is not so, for if their alcoholism is arrested, they continue to behave in the same way, and to get into very nearly the same kind of trouble, sober, that used to be explained by their drunkenness. More frequently, however, their alcoholism cannot be arrested by any means whatever, even when they seem to be trying to co-operate to the best of their ability. They make up a good percentage of the so-called "recalcitrant alcoholics": the ones who do well for short periods, then relapse, then return to their effort with no apparent regret or worry over the relapse, continuing this pattern indefinitely. Their emotional equipment seems to be extremely abnormal, and their sense of right and wrong practically nonexistent. Medical science has so far given us no answer to the terrible problem of the psychopathic personality, with or without alcoholism. In one case the family, having tried everything known without success, finally resorted to "psychiatric surgery"—in this case the brain operation known as the topectomy. But this, too, failed and the only release proved to be death. *The Story of Mrs. Murphy*, a novel which was widely publicized as being the story of an alcoholic, is actually the story of a psychopathic personality, with alcoholic drinking as one of the symptoms of this condition. If the main character's alcoholism had by any remote chance been arrested, there is little doubt that he would have continued his abnormal life regardless, for even in his occasionally quite long sober periods, his behavior and reactions were highly abnormal.

This group, then, whom I call the mentally ill drinkers, are alcoholics, and more. They are actually suffering from a mental or nervous disorder, with alcoholic drinking as one of their symptoms. They cannot be handled as one might handle a true alcoholic; and they should not be handled at all by the non-professional. They should be taken quickly to a good physician or psychiatrist for diagnosis and advice on what course to pursue. It is dangerous for the amateur would-be helper to get involved in these cases, for he can often do more harm than good.

The same advice could be given regarding the "feeble-minded drinker," though it would hardly seem to be necessary. These unfortunate people are too obviously what they are, whether drinking or not, to need explanation. Where alcoholic drinking is added to their already difficult condition, it becomes a matter for trained professional aid. No amateur can hope to solve their problem.

4

WHO IS NOT AN ALCOHOLIC?

Current estimates indicate that there are approximately 70,000,000 Americans who drink. These drinkers can be divided into many different groups. There are the "sometime drinkers," who very occasionally take a drink, perhaps only two or three times a year. There are the "moderate drinkers," who drink on occasions when drinking is in order, but never more than one or at most two drinks. Included in this group are those who like wine with their meals, but rarely drink cocktails or highballs; those who enjoy beer, but only occasionally take anything stronger; and those who for years have enjoyed one cocktail before dinner as a regular, almost a ritualistic, procedure. The "social drinkers" can be described as those who do not limit their consumption, but who follow whatever the general trend may be, including occasional heavy drinking at parties or on evenings when drinking is the main diversion: they rarely drink to drunkenness, although they may quite frequently get "mellow," or "tight," or "high." They often go for days or weeks without drinking at all. All of these groups are so obviously nonalcoholic drinkers that they should not need any further elaboration.

There are two more groups of nonalcoholic drinkers, however, whose drinking is not so easy to distinguish from alcoholic drinking. Both of them cause confusion in the minds of observers, and even sometimes in their own minds. They are the "heavy drinkers" and the "occasional drunks."

Heavy drinkers are no phenomenon in our day and age. There are a great many of them, especially in the big cities, and they number women in their ranks as well as men. They are the drinkers who more often than not have several cocktails before lunch, who think that four, five or more drinks before dinner is nothing, and who continue drinking through dinner and on through the evening most nights of the week. They usually go to bed a little "high," and sometimes quite drunk, especially on weekends, when they are apt to drink considerably more than is their wont during the week. Drinking is obviously a very important part of their lives: many of them have said that life would be impossibly dull without it; that it is the source of most fun, and they couldn't possibly have a good time without drinking; that it makes everyone better company; and that it is an essential to good entertaining. The cocktail party is a major source of diversion to heavy drinkers, and not infrequently is stretched on well into the evening, with dinner finally being eaten at ten, eleven or even later at night. Some heavy drinkers occasionally exhibit a few of the early and middle behavior symptoms of alcoholism, thus heightening the confusion regarding their status.

There are important distinctions which can be made, however, to help clarify the difference between heavy drinking and alcoholic drinking. It has been said, time and again, that there is but the thinnest line dividing these two things, and that it is almost impossible to tell when that line has been crossed; and that in other cases, one cannot say who is on one side and who is on the other. This does not seem to me to be true, for two reasons.

First, in heavy drinking, progression is not shown. Many heavy drinkers appear to stand precisely still for fifteen, twenty, twenty-five and more years of drinking, with the same amount of drinking producing generally the same effects. Almost anyone can point to some drinker they have known, who has consistently drunk much more than is considered "social drinking" over an indefinite period of years, and who has not lost everything and slid down the incline of alcoholism. These drinkers may have hurt their health and/or their career, but it has usually been an invisible hurt, not directly attributable to their drinking, although that may actually be the root of it. In many other heavy drinkers the progressive element marking alcoholism is actually reversed: they gradually cut down their consumption as they grow older, almost unconsciously and with no apparent effort to do so. People who were definitely heavy drinkers in their twenties and early thirties, for instance, very often change to social or even moderate drinking as they approach and enter their forties. This is not usually noticed as such: it is regarded merely as a part of a broader change, and spoken of as "settling down" or "getting in the groove" of work, or of life generally.

Second, the element of choice exists for the heavy drinker: he is able to control his drinking if and when he wishes. In the case of a physical ailment, for instance, if the doctor advises cutting his consumption to so many drinks per day or week, he is capable of doing this, as well as being able to cut it out completely for any specified period of time without any deep discomfort (even though there may be extreme annoyance or grumbling). In the case of a new job, too, the heavy drinker may find it politic to cut his drinking way down, and quietly do so. Vanity, too, will sometimes provide the reason for tightening the reins, particularly if losing weight is the desired objective. In any case, countless heavy drinkers have drastically reduced the amount they once normally consumed, for any one of these and many other reasons. The point is that they were able to do this at will, and without serious difficulties. Furthermore, the heavy drinker only rarely transgresses the rules of any particular occasion by getting drunk at the wrong time or place. He chooses his time, his place, and his drinking companions pretty carefully.

I have personally observed a great many instances of heavy drinking over a long period of years, which confirm my belief that there is a distinct and identifiable line between such heavy drinking and alcoholic drinking. Living in New York in the last few years of the Twenties, I had a wide acquaintanceship, most of whom were extremely heavy drinkers. I also appeared to be just that.

Actually, however, I was already showing many signs of early alcoholism, although neither I nor anyone else recognized them. I went abroad to live in 1930, and there my progression in alcoholism continued, with a complete breakdown coming in 1936. My own recovery took place in 1939, and I returned to live and work in New York, where gradually I met once again many of my old acquaintances of the Twenties. Some of them were still drinking exactly as they had when I had first known them, with no visible harmful effects. The majority, however, today drink comparatively little—at most, social drinking in the strictest sense of the term. None that I have met again has stopped drinking entirely—and none has become an alcoholic.

It has been my experience, working in the field of alcoholism, that many heavy drinkers, and even social drinkers, are sometimes concerned about their own drinking. To such people, and to any alcoholics who may exist among them, unknown to themselves or anyone else, I would say only this:

Ponder the symptoms given here, and test them out against yourself. Try your control against your drinking. If you are not an alcoholic you are bound to win. Many people do this for the assurance it gives them that they are safe to continue enjoying a drink when they want one. Don't make the mistake of testing yourself by "going on the wagon." That is no test, because even the most advanced alcoholic can sometimes do that for quite a considerable time. The test, to have any real validity, must be of controlled drinking, since alcoholism is identified by drinking which has got out of control.

There is a simple test which has been used hundreds of times for this purpose. Even an extremely heavy drinker should have no trouble in passing it, whereas an alcoholic, if able to complete it at all, could do so only under such heavy pressure that his life would be more miserable than he thinks it would be if he stopped drinking altogether. The chances are a hundred to one, however, against a true alcoholic's being either willing or able to undertake the test.

The Test: Select any time at all for instituting it. Now is the best time. For the next six months *at least,* decide that you will stick to a certain number of drinks a day, that number to be not less than one and not more than three. If you are not a daily drinker, then the test should be the stated number of drinks from one to three, on those days when you do drink. Some heavy drinkers confine their drinking to weekends, but still worry about the amount they consume then. Whatever number you choose must not be exceeded under any circumstances whatever, and this includes weddings, births, funerals, occasions of sudden death and disaster, unexpected or long-awaited inheritance, promotion, or other happy events, reunions or meetings with old friends or good customers, or just sheer boredom. There must also be no special occasions on which you feel justified in adding to your quota of the stated number of drinks, such as a severe emotional upset, or the appointment to close the biggest deal of your career, or the audition you've been waiting for all your life, or the meeting with someone who is crucial to your future and of whom you are terrified. Absolutely no exceptions, or the test has been failed.

This is not an easy test, but it has been passed handily by any number of drinkers who wished to show themselves, or their families and friends, that they were not compulsive drinkers. If by any chance they failed the test, showing that they were alcoholics, they showed themselves, too, that they were, whether they were then ready to admit it openly or not. At least it prepared them for such an admission, and for the constructive action which normally follows that admission.

It is important to add that observers of such tests should not use them to try to force a flunkee to premature action. This may well backfire and produce a stubborn determination on the part of the one who has been unable to pass the test, to prove that it is not alcoholism that caused the failure. He can and does do this in several ways: by stopping drinking altogether for a self-specified time (when this is over he usually breaks out in even worse form than before, and with an added resentment toward those who "drove" him to it); by instituting a rigid control over his own drinking, which produces a constant irritability that makes him impossible to be with, coupled with periodic outbreaks of devastating nature; or by giving himself a very large quota and insisting that he has remained within it, even when he has obviously been too drunk to remember how many drinks he had. In extreme cases, he may even give himself a quota of so many drinks, and take them straight from the bottle, calling each bottle "the" drink. The backfiring from too great outside pressure may also cause a complete collapse: knowing and admitting that he cannot pass the test and is therefore an alcoholic, he will resist efforts to force him to take action by saying in effect, "So I'm an alcoholic, so I can't control my drinking, so I'll drink as I must," and go all out for perdition. This last, despite the expressed concern of some people (who believe that admitting alcoholism to be a disease, and alcoholic drinking to be uncontrollable drinking, is simply to give alcoholics a good excuse to continue), very rarely happens. Nevertheless the possibility must be taken into account by those who are trying to help an alcoholic to recognize his trouble and take constructive action on it. If he is left alone after failing such a self-taken test, the failure will begin to work on him—it has planted a seed of knowledge which may well grow into action.

The "occasional drunk" usually comes from the ranks of heavy drinkers, sometimes social drinkers. Rarely is he an abstainer between his bouts, as is generally the case with periodic alcoholics. Sometimes called "spree drinkers," these are the ones who every now and then deliberately indulge in short periods of drinking to drunkenness, usually at sporadic intervals. They talk of the "good" it does them to have a "purge" once in a while, or to "let down their hair" or to "kick over the traces" and have "all-out fun." Unfortunately for them they sometimes get into trouble during these sprees, and their drinking habits are thus brought to public attention. But they can and do stop such indulgences if they find it is costing them too much, for their sprees are their idea of fun, and not a necessity. "Occasional drunks" are most often found among youthful drinkers, whose ideas of "fun," for one reason or another, have come to center around drinking and the uninhibited behavior which excessive drinking allows.

There are a few points I would like to make about heavy drinking, which have been hinted at in the foregoing. While it is not alcoholism, and may be defined as "excessive drinking by choice," it can be harmful in a number of ways. It is a curious fact that alcoholic drinking does not seem seriously to impair the physical health of the drinker in any of the ways one might expect. (This is leaving out the group scientifically defined as "alcoholics with complications," *i.e.*, those who, through prolonged alcoholism, have finally been physically and/or mentally damaged. It has been estimated [1] that in 1955 there were 4,712,000 alcoholics, of whom one quarter, or 1,178,000, were alcoholics with complications.) Among the thousands of alcoholics who are today recovered, very few have had stomach ailments (ulcers, gastritis, etc.), liver involvements (cirrhosis, for instance), kidney or heart trouble, neuritis or neuralgia. But among heavy drinkers one will find these ailments widespread. The theory has been advanced (not too seriously) by recovered alcoholics themselves that perhaps alcoholism, in involving their nervous systems and mental processes, skipped over their physical organs. Whatever the reason, it appears true that nonalcoholic, but heavy, drinkers damage their physical health by their drinking much more often than do alcoholics. Particularly they seem

---

[1] "Alcoholism: Nature and Extent of the Problem," Mark Keller, *The Annals of the American Academy of Political and Social Science*, January 1958, p. 6.

more prone than other people to stomach, liver and kidney ailments, and various forms of neuritis. And since they like drinking the way they do, and want to continue it, they will always search for other reasons to explain the ailment (which usually exist, for there are nearly always several possible medical reasons); and other ways than cutting down or cutting out their drinking, to overcome it (which also exist, but alone are not usually enough). Nevertheless the fact must be faced: that heavy drinking can be among the things which are harmful to the health, even when it does not in itself cause a continuing problem in the life.

A perfect example is the case of Ted P., who has been a heavy drinker for twenty-eight of his forty-five years, with no progression whatever, and no apparent harm to his life in general. He suffers, however, from a recurrent stomach ailment which causes him great pain every few years. Each time an attack comes on, his doctors give him the same orders—no drinking—in addition to other treatment. Each time he follows the orders meticulously, grumbling loudly, and after some months is allowed to drink a restricted amount for another period, which again he follows meticulously. The attack being pronounced over, he immediately resumes his usual heavy drinking. Does it not seem reasonable to suppose that if he cut out drinking entirely, or at least remained permanently on the restricted consumption (which is actually moderate drinking) allowed during his convalescent periods, he *might* avoid any future attacks?

Heavy drinking may also be harmful to the career without being alcoholism. In this case it is not the drinking per se that does the harm, but the results of that drinking. People who normally drink heavily, usually do so on a near-daily basis. There are two ways in which this practice can, and too often does, hurt their work. Several cocktails before lunch means a fair amount of alcohol in the system—enough to be felt at any rate. Alcohol being technically an anesthetic, or sedative, it acts like other depressants, not in making one depressed, but in lulling one's inhibitions, thoughts and emotions. It is well known that the highest functions of the brain are the first to be affected: among these are judgment and clarity of thought. The individual who has dulled his faculties of thought and judgment in the middle of the day by even an ounce or two of alcohol, is obviously not as fit for his afternoon's work as he was in the morning: he cannot think as quickly or as clearly, nor is his judgment at its normal pitch. He has, in short, slowed down. This may not be noticeable in any way, but it can not help affecting the quality of work he produces in the long run, so that he may not go as far as he would have with his full faculties going full bent throughout the working day. Besides, his morning's work may already have been affected by his heavy drinking the night before, and this is the second way such drinking can hurt his career. While heavy drinkers rarely suffer the epic hangovers of the alcoholic, they do know what a hangover means, and usually feel one, however slight, after having been even a bit "tight" the night before. Few heavy drinkers ever take a drink in the morning to get going (although there are exceptions to this as to everything concerning drinking habits); they "work off" the feeling, or suffer it through till their lunchtime drinks. But no one's mental (or physical) processes can be considered up to par while he is feeling the effects of a hangover, any more than while he is suffering from a heavy cold, or a severe headache, or a stomach upset. Feeling ill also slows a person down, both physically and mentally. No one knows, for instance, how many industrial accidents could be traced to the slowed-down reactions of a worker who was suffering from the physical and mental effects of a hangover, nor how many automobile accidents have a similar origin. But quite apart from obvious disasters like these, it can be said that anyone who is suffering the effects of a hangover, even if he does not feel them strongly, is not able to function to the best of his normal capacity. And if he suffers these effects with any frequency, his work is bound to be affected. Once again, he may not go as far in his work as he could have with his faculties at their best.

It is not easy to find examples to prove these points, and possibly one example will not be sufficient proof to most readers. Nevertheless Fred S. offers an indication of the truth of the previous statements. He had been a heavy drinker for seventeen years with no progression and no visible bad effects. Then he married a girl who did not like to drink, and at the same time his job took him to a new community—and new friends. During the last thirteen of those seventeen years of heavy drinking he had held the same job: that of a salesman. He had done neither better nor worse than his fellow salesmen, excepting that he had been kept on all through the depression, indicating that his company felt he had better potentialities than others whose records seemed as good as his. But after this one sign of preference, he seemed to sink into a rut, maintaining the same pace of work he had shown from the beginning—until his move to new territory. His sales began to mount, and within a year he was promoted to Sales Manager. Two years later he became a Vice-President, and today is in line to head up his company. What that company did not know was that his wife's lack of interest in drinking had done two things: cut down his own daily consumption, and gradually changed his social life and companions. This last was made easier and quicker by their change of location. One other factor was that Fred was approaching his forties, the time when many heavy drinkers begin to change their drinking habits. One can not state as a fact that the change in drinking habits was alone responsible for Fred's rise in business. Both his marriage and the change in territory must be taken into account, as well as his age and the length of time he had served his firm. But there seems little doubt that the difference in his drinking helped, and may well have been the major factor.

Despite these warnings of the sometimes harmful effects of heavy drinking, there would seem to be no real reason for fear. It should be remembered that, where no progression is shown, and the power of choice remains, it is within the drinker's power to change his drinking habits should they disturb him. The danger signal goes up only when an individual knows that his way of drinking is disturbing some department of his life, and fails to do anything about it. In such cases the possibility of alcoholism is very real.

Knowledge about alcoholism can thus be seen to have very great value for all drinkers, but particularly for social and heavy drinkers, even if they do not personally know an alcoholic. If they can be sure that they are not risking alcoholism, are showing no signs of it, they should be able to enjoy their chosen way of drinking without worry. If their way of drinking is causing them any concern whatsoever, they would be doing themselves a great service by learning to place it in its proper category, and dealing with it accordingly.

We have seen that many alcoholics seem unable or unwilling to admit to alcoholism with any ease. The same is true with some heavy drinkers, who insist in the face of contradictory facts that they are mild social drinkers, or even moderate drinkers with a very occasional spillover. Why should there be this peculiar delusion with regard to ways of drinking?

In the case of alcoholics it is not so difficult to explain. The stigma attached to alcoholism has had terrible repercussions in chaining alcoholics to their condition. It should be understandable that no man or woman is eager to admit to a lack of will power or character which is considered a shameful weakness by his fellows. And he is equally unwilling to admit that he deliberately abuses a privilege which his friends would not think of abusing. Alcoholics will insist to the bitter end that they "can take it or leave it alone" just like their nonalcoholic friends. They do not want to be "different"—which is a very human reaction. And, of course, most of them haven't the faintest idea that alcoholism is a disease over which they, unaided, have only the slightest control, if any, and for which complete cessation of drinking is the only safe answer. Therefore they cling to the hope that they can be like other people again, and eagerly embrace individual opinions that some particular outside factor in their lives is responsible for their "temporary" loss of control. They want desperately to believe that they will be able to return to controlled drinking "like other people."

Why heavy drinkers are sometimes equally unwilling to admit to the actual heaviness of their drinking, is not so simple to see. In all probability the major reason lies in their confusion as to what alcoholism is, and whether or not they might be considered alcoholic drinkers or "weaklings," if the full story were known. There seems little doubt that if the heavy drinker is truly so dependent on the amount he drinks that he cannot face even the thought of cutting it down, he is in danger of alcoholism. In such a case the full facts would probably show that his drinking had indeed shown progression. It is reasonable to assume that, in the case of those heavy drinkers who wilfully and obviously conceal the facts about how much and how often they drink, refusing to admit the truth, there are doubts as to their true status. They may well be alcoholics with an unusually slow progression of the illness. The heavy drinker who is just that, need have no fear of admitting it: it is not a serious condition, and he is able to master it if and when he wishes.

In point of fact there need be no fear of drinking as such. Science has ruled alcohol out as "the" cause of alcoholism. The world knows, because it can see with its own eyes, that occasional, moderate social drinking does not disrupt people's lives. Heavy drinking cannot be given such a complete bill of health, but it need not be feared by anyone in full possession of the facts. Fears about drinking, and the violent prejudices that the pros and cons of drinking have aroused through the years, could be largely done away with if knowledge of the facts was widespread.

5

HOW CAN I BE SURE THAT X IS REALLY AN ALCOHOLIC?

Most people think this is very easy. It isn't. Certainly it is easy to spot an advanced alcoholic, but by that time it is not usually easy to approach him helpfully, or to handle the situation created by his alcoholism in a constructive and helpful manner. As a matter of cold fact, by this time most people are only concerned with ways and means of avoiding said drunk. All they want is to wash their hands of him completely, and to be allowed to forget that he and his problems exist. Excepting, always, some long-suffering wives and mothers. Husbands, incidentally, do not often stick up to this stage.

In the case of people very close to an alcoholic, the preceding chapters should have provided a guide. Even in the closest relationship, however, caution is necessary. It is fatal to jump to conclusions and act hastily where an alcoholic is concerned. And no matter how clear the signs may seem, it must be remembered that time is necessary to provide the distinction between alcoholism and heavy drinking. Where progression and loss of control are not clearly shown, there is no ground for drawing a conclusion. This makes it extremely difficult for those who do not actually live with the person suspected of alcoholism, to be sure of their ground.

Nevertheless, drinking behavior and other behavior, plus certain psychological signs, can be evaluated by an informed person. It is noticeable, for instance, if someone almost always continues to drunkenness when drinking. It is even noticeable if one drinker in the crowd consistently finishes his drink well ahead of the others, gradually drawing ahead in consumption. It is noticeable if a drinker is continually "going on the wagon" for short periods, or constantly talking about "going on the wagon" at a future date which never seems to arrive. It is noticeable if a drinker displays marked "Jekyll and Hyde" characteristics when drinking, such as a normally quiet and reserved person who becomes loud, argumentative, belligerent or violent, only when drinking . . . or the converse where a usually alert and intelligent person becomes morose and silent, or appears to be in a waking coma. In short, drinking behavior provides the most obvious signs to an informed onlooker who does not live with the alcoholic.

There are other behavior and psychological signs, however, not necessarily connected with drinking periods, which can be evaluated. Recurrent periods of tension, which show themselves as extreme irritability, flashes of temper, unreasonable ideas, and a general attitude of resentment toward the world, are noticeable. A tendency to make mountains out of molehills, creating scenes in which the alcoholic marches off in a huff, or announces his intention of getting good and drunk because of the episode, can also be observed by outsiders. Often these latter signs are noticed by the friends of an alcoholic, without in any way being associated with drinking. They merely consider so-and-so to be a difficult person, "terribly touchy," or "getting impossible to be with."

A case in point was that of Harriet J., a talented artist whose friends very rarely saw her drink too much. She talked quite frequently about going on the wagon, and once or twice did so for very short periods, to the amazement of her companions, who could not see why she should bother when she drank so little. Her business dealings had long been stormy because of her temperamental outbursts, usually defended by admirers of her work as due to her "artistic temperament." Finally her difficult and unpredictable behavior began to invade her social life, and friends dropped away. Nevertheless it came as a startling surprise to all who knew her when she suddenly announced that she was an alcoholic and had stopped drinking entirely. It seemed that one of her most noticeable tendencies, that of creating a scene out of nothing and leaving the party in a huff, had been for the purpose of getting away where she could complete her drinking to drunkenness, unobserved. Her daytime or business behavior was largely the result of appalling hangovers or of the terrible fight to control her desperate need for drinks.

Freed of drinking, she behaved as normally as anyone else.

It is true that various forms of difficult behavior, and psychological signs of inner disturbance also occur in many nondrinkers, "sometime drinkers," moderate or social drinkers, in which case they obviously are not signs of impending or early alcoholism. For this reason, it is not wise for an onlooker to seek to identify alcoholism except through drinking behavior. When this is noticeable and accompanied by other behavior and psychological symptoms, he can begin to form an opinion.

Even here one may run into an exceptionally heavy drinker who, on short observance, seems to be teetering on the edge of alcoholism. Only time will show the difference, for if, over a period of years, no progression whatever is to be seen, the drinker cannot truly be called an alcoholic. Such drinkers are sometimes doing obvious harm to themselves by the amount they drink, and so are a matter of great concern to their families and friends. Suggesting to them that they are alcoholics, or even in danger of becoming alcoholics, is not generally very successful. The approach to such a person should be as cautious and as carefully worked out as if he were an alcoholic, but there are vital differences. In heavy drinking success can be achieved by diversion: finding new interests, or a valid reason for cutting consumption. A doctor in whom the heavy drinker has confidence can frequently persuade him to limit his drinking; even a friend for whom he has respect and admiration can help. The biggest difference is that the heavy drinker need only be persuaded to cut down his drinking; if he can be convinced and made to want to do this, it is possible for him: he need not give it up entirely. This makes the problem very much easier than if he were an alcoholic, and had to face the inevitability of giving up drinking altogether.

George B. was an exceptionally heavy drinker whose family and friends were deeply concerned because of its effect on his health. He had a kidney ailment, and while the doctors had not forbidden him to drink, they were apparently unaware of his outsize consumption. Pleas from his family had no effect: he answered reasonably enough that his drinking wasn't giving any real trouble, and he was sure his kidney would give trouble anyway. One of George's friends was an accomplished amateur flier, who, after long trying, finally managed to get George to fly with him. It was a case of love at first sight, and George started learning to fly on weekends, with an immediate cessation of weekend drinking. Not long after, his family realized that he was drinking very little at any time. When they mentioned it, expressing their delight, George simply said he "couldn't do both and flying was more fun." Whether this meant physically (co-ordination, speed of reactions, general fitness) or financially, he did not say. And no one cared, least of all George.

Another problem an observer can run into is the situational drinker. This does not actually present a problem which the observer need solve, however, since the situational drinker requires the same kind of outside help as the alcoholic. The main thing for the observer to remember, especially if he is a would-be helper, is that situational drinking is indistinguishable from alcoholic drinking, and must be treated in exactly the same way. If, therefore, the observer knows of some tragic background to the drinking, which in his opinion explains it perfectly, that does not mean the drinker should be treated any differently: it is still necessary to get him to seek treatment and to stop drinking, even though the particular nature of his drinking problem may allow him to resume social drinking at a much later time. The behavior of the would-be helper toward the situational drinker, then, should be identical with that toward an alcoholic.

In most cases the observer is going to suspect alcoholism long before he is sure, and if he wishes to be helpful, he is going to have to bide his time, with patience. He should give the suspect opportunities to show his status more clearly, both by watching his drinking behavior when possible, and by listening sympathetically (for he can learn much of the presence of the listed psychological symptoms by listening). The word "sympathetically" is all-important. If the observer is to be of any help when the time is ripe, he must take care to avoid raising any barriers of suspicion. He must not lecture or condemn—he must be careful that what he considers "sweet reasonableness" is not construed as interference, or no help can afterwards be given because it will not be acceptable from that source.

Lyman T. illustrates the value of forbearance in such circumstances. For fifteen years his friends watched him descend slowly but surely into the abyss of alcoholism. His wife left him. Many of his friends deserted him. Some remained, for his native sweetness and charm were very great despite his irresponsible behavior. One of those remaining, Dick, was a self-confessed alcoholic who had stopped drinking ten years before. How he had done this was so personal to him, however, that he was not able to pass it on to Lyman. Dick then consulted his friend Bob, who had also stopped drinking, but with the help of Alcoholics Anonymous, and brought him to meet Lyman. It was obvious that Lyman had no intention, at that time, of taking any action. Dick and Bob discussed the problem, and with their special insights as recovered alcoholics, recognized that they must make no further overt move. They settled back to wait, meanwhile maintaining a warm friendship with Lyman and freely discussing alcoholism as a disease whenever possible. Other friends pressed them for action, especially on several occasions when Lyman was so ill it seemed he could not survive. Fortunately he had an income, so that his inability to work did not prevent funds being available for medical attention when necessary. Five years after their first meeting, Lyman asked Bob if he could talk to him seriously. It was the first step toward what has so far been a good recovery. Both Dick and Bob are sure that if either of them had used any undue pressure, Lyman would still be drinking—or dead. They are equally sure that their frequent discussions of all sides of alcoholism, and methods of treating it, had great bearing on Lyman's eventual decision to take action. Bob in particular is convinced that his own natural attitude of sympathetic understanding is the reason Lyman sought his help.

It is to be fervently hoped that all would-be helpers do not have to sit by and observe years of progressive deterioration before they can make a constructive move. If they are certain that their particular suspect is in real danger—is actually an alcoholic—they should seek ways of reaching him with the basic information on alcoholism. Such information as is contained here, for instance, particularly since it is not directed straight at him, like a noose waiting to slip down over his head, might show him the way. Information should always be presented as a matter of general interest to everyone, not just to one suspected of alcoholism. The attitude of those discussing the subject of drinking and particularly alcoholic drinking should be casual but sympathetic, full of interest but not personal, aware of the deep problems involved, but not taking any emotional stand on them. There must be no righteous indignation, no horrified disbelief, no shame, no condemnation. Sympathetic understanding and a firm belief in the necessity of taking constructive action, plus a conviction that such action can be successful, are keys which may unlock the door to the alcoholic's deep-seated desire to know what it is that is really wrong with him. In fact, the effort to impart information on alcoholism may well be the means of finding out whether the suspect is actually an alcoholic or not. It may allow him to express freely his own inner concern about his drinking, which may thus be constructively discussed, without emotion, recriminations, or contempt. Experience has shown that these are the only conditions under which a suspected alcoholic will discuss his problem. The difficulty has been that there were not enough people with sufficient knowledge to give them an objective attitude, and, even more important, an attitude of sympathetic understanding.

6

THE "HOME TREATMENT"

While it is true that alcoholics can recover, it is also true that in order to do so they need first to know what ails them, second what to do about it, and third, to do it. In this they are just like other sick people. We do not expect someone who appears to be suffering from an illness to diagnose and treat himself, unaided. We do expect him to seek expert advice from qualified sources, and we hope that he will then follow that advice, knowing that in the end his recovery depends on his own co-operation. In many cases of all sorts of illnesses, it has been necessary for the sick person's family to seek advice first, and then to bring their patient to the point of co-operating. The way they go about this always has great bearing on whether or not they succeed, no matter what the illness may be.

The "Home Treatment" is the title ironically given by some students of alcoholism to the methods frequently used by desperate and harassed families who are trying "to bring (their alcoholic) to his senses." Unfortunately these are methods which almost inevitably aggravate the condition they are intended to alleviate. But since countless families use them, obviously without realizing that they are thus defeating their own ends, it should be helpful to point them out. This chapter might well be entitled "What *Not* to Do if You Have an Alcoholic in Your Home." No blame should be attached to people who in their desperate need have resorted to these methods. They are a natural outcome of the general belief that alcoholic drinking is merely a question of "will power," and therefore entirely within the control of the alcoholic *if* he could just be made to exercise that control. Such methods have usually been honest efforts to make him do so.

The "home treatment" can be generally divided into two main categories: words and actions, or talk and behavior. Talk usually goes on for some time before behavior begins to bear it out, and then it continues right alongside the behavior. For purposes of clarity we will follow the line of talk through to its bitter end before taking up the behavior which usually joins it midway.

Talk, to someone whose drinking is beginning to create a problem, usually begins with "sweet reasonableness." An effort is made at friendly discussion on what drinking is doing to the drinker (such as his "lack of judgment" and "thoughtlessness"), leading up to what it is doing to his family, at which point it is apt to become a trifle acid, and sometimes to end in an all-out row. Nevertheless the effort to discuss the matter "reasonably" is renewed over and over again, despite the fact that as time goes on it seems to lead more and more swiftly to acrimonious dispute or cold anger. The alcoholic soon calls this nagging, and uses it as an excuse to drink more, not less. It is not suggested here that friendly discussion should be avoided, but merely that a constant repetition of an effort which is obviously bringing no results is not only useless, but can backfire, making the situation even more difficult. Also, such discussions sometimes call for and produce promises, which are not kept, and this leads to accusations and bitterness.

Emotional appeals are another form of talk frequently used. "How can you do this to me?", "Doesn't my love mean anything to you?", "How can you do this to the children" or "to yourself?" These point the finger of shame and blame at the alcoholic, increasing his already acute sense of guilt, and giving him another excuse to drink more, in order to "forget." The same result usually follows the "morality lecture" method, typified by such statements as "Where is your self-respect?", "Have you no sense of decency?", or "I should think you would die of shame—a man of your background" or "Where is your will power—be a man," etc., etc. Neither the emotional appeal nor the morality lecture ever seems to do the slightest good in bringing an alcoholic to seek help. On the contrary, it usually drives him further behind a wall of defiance, from which vantage point he regards the people who talk that way with growing resentment and suspicion.

Promises and coaxing sometimes appear to have a temporary success, but it rarely lasts long. "I'll promise never to mention it again, if you——," or "We'll go on the wagon together. Let's promise. Come on, please . . .", or "Promise you won't drink more than I do—drink for drink," or even "Give it up, for me. I'll do anything you like, in return." These place an added burden on the alcoholic, who is literally unable to fulfill his part of the bargain, even when he desperately wants to. Often, after trying for a while, he will explode in a binge, leading to recriminations, anger and further resentment.

Threats are equally useless when they are not carried out. "I'm going to leave you if you go on like this," or "I'm going to go to your boss and tell him what it's really like—maybe *he* can influence you," or "I'm going to commit you to an institution—you're crazy," or "If you do this again, I'm going to call the police." It is not suggested that doing any of these things instead of threatening to do them is the right answer—it is merely pointed out that threats, as such, very rarely achieve good results. They too can boomerang, driving the alcoholic further from the reach of the threatener, strengthening his wall of defiance, increasing his resentment and suspicion.

The behavior which is a part of the "home treatment" does not generally begin until the talking has progressed well beyond sweet reasonableness and emotional appeals. It is apt to start with not keeping up the home supply of liquor, "forgetting" to reorder. Since the alcoholic finds a way to remedy this immediately, by bringing in his own supply, it is soon succeeded by hiding the bottles, perhaps hoping that if they are not seen they will not be thought of. The main purpose in hiding the liquor, however, is to prevent the "sneaking" of drinks. This rarely succeeds for two reasons: first, by the time this is resorted to, the alcoholic has already taken to hiding his own extra supply for just such purposes, so that nothing results but a double game of hide-and-seek. Second, if he should run out of his own, he can still usually find the bottle hidden by the family. Alcoholics as a rule are extraordinarily good at this sort of thing—and even enjoy the excitement of the hunt.

Some families lock up the liquor, instead of hiding it. This is apt to produce a more violent and unpleasant reaction from the alcoholic, since it rubs his sensitivity about his own drinking on its rawest spot. And if he has consumed his own hidden supply, and needs or desperately wants a drink, he is apt to resort to extreme measures to get it: jimmying locks, breaking doors, or devising ingenious stratagems to get the liquor hideaway unlocked. In other words, if the alcoholic needs or wants a drink, he will get it no matter what devices the family has thought up to keep it from him. There is only one thing they can do, and this is often the next step in behavior; pouring all liquor in the house down the sink. Once again, however, this usually proves a futile gesture, for the alcoholic then sets his really remarkable ingenuity to getting more in, or to getting himself out of the house, and to the nearest source of supply. It must be remembered that, to him, his need is desperate and overwhelming; it brooks no interference, and sets up in him the blind courage of a charging bull, plus all the cunning and cleverness of a skilled second-story man. Generally speaking, the frantic and upset family is no match for him at such times. Their genuine efforts to do what they think will help him, will "save him from himself," only succeed in driving him further from them, thus making it more difficult for them to be really helpful if and when they find out what they can and should do.

One other method of behavior is often used where it is possible: withholding money. This is more frequently possible where the alcoholic is a woman, and sometimes goes further than not allowing her to handle cash. Numerous instances have been cited where the family instructed shops and stores as to what could or could not be charged to the account. Wives and mothers have been known to ask the local tavern owner or bartender not to give credit to their alcoholic, sometimes even going so far as to report taverns to the authorities for serving their alcoholic "when he was already intoxicated." If the situation has reached this point, consultation with expert opinion is long overdue, for the alcoholic is far gone and badly in need of treatment. The methods described are not treatment, and are doomed to failure insofar as helping the alcoholic is concerned.

There are occasions where the family's behavior extends outside the family circle, where they ask their friends to help, by not serving liquor when they are there, or by offering the alcoholic only a nonalcoholic drink. The resentment occasioned in the alcoholic by this knows no bounds, and often pushes the situation right out of hand. One alcoholic woman of my acquaintance said that the worst binge of her drinking career followed a dinner party at which the host, passing the cocktails, remarked in what seemed to her a hideously silent room, "The grapefruit juice on the end is yours." She took it, writhing in humiliation, refused to speak to her husband when they got home, and was drunk for a month thereafter. Almost every alcoholic has had some experience of the "home treatment." Those who have recovered look back on it as among the great setbacks to their own efforts to handle their problem. Johnny K., a filling station attendant with five children, expresses it for many of them: "I knew something was wrong and it worried me, but my wife went on at me so that I had to defend myself. I really loved her and the kids, and I knew I wasn't bad, but what she said made me sound that way, and she nagged about it till I thought I'd go nuts. I had to drink to get away from it. Then when she began hiding my liquor and counting out pennies to me from my own pay check, I really got sore. I know now she was trying to help me, but it sure didn't look like it to me then—it just made me worse."

There is a great deal the family can do to help the alcoholic make a start toward recovery. Their own attitude toward him and his problem is often the key. And if they are properly informed as to the nature of alcoholism and what it does to the alcoholic, a sympathetic, understanding, and constructive attitude should not be too difficult to attain. There is no question that in most cases it will pay dividends, for alcoholics generally respond gratefully to warmth and understanding, just as they respond resentfully to what they consider criticism and censure.

7

ALCOHOLICS CAN RECOVER

There is an old saw, "Once a drunk, always a drunk," which is still far too widely believed. It has played its destructive part in the prevention of constructive action on alcoholism far too long. No one can guess how often it has helped to clamp the irons of stigma and shame to an alcoholic who, with a little encouragement and help, might have made a comeback.

Regardless of what the true causes of alcoholism may be, there can be no question as to the effect environment can have on alcoholics. Environment is a broad word, but for our purposes it has at least three components: geographical, human and mental. The environment which has the greatest effect on alcoholics is that resulting from the combination of these, which together, make up the *mental climate*, or atmosphere, in which the alcoholic lives. Of necessity he shares that atmosphere with the people who create it: his family, friends, neighbors and fellow workers. And like them he responds to that atmosphere, living comfortably in accord with it, or miserably in opposition to it. By the nature of his illness, the alcoholic finds himself most of the time in opposition to the atmosphere surrounding him, and he reacts to this by claiming that the world around him "does not understand him" (or his problem). As a matter of fact, in this he is right. The world surrounding the alcoholic has, until very recently, rarely understood him, or what ailed him, or what to do about it. The prevailing mental climate of ignorance, misconception, and prejudice concerning alcoholism has not been a healthy climate for the growth and spread of recoveries; it has been a climate which fostered the monstrous growth of alcoholism itself.

If we are ever to bring alcoholism under control, as we have other scourges of mankind, we must change that climate. We must create a mental climate of knowledge and understanding which will affect the alcoholic constructively, bringing him first to a recognition of his illness, and second to a recognition of his need and his right—in fact his moral obligation—to seek treatment for that illness. This is precisely what we have done for tuberculosis and are trying to do for cancer. In the case of alcoholism there are two particular periods in the alcoholic's career when the effect of the mental climate in which he lives is of vital importance. The first is the period when his alcoholism is beginning to show and the second is when he is making his initial efforts to recover.

In the first instance, when the early signs of alcoholism are becoming noticeable, it is important to remember that the alcoholic shares the mental climate of those around him—*including* the ignorance, misconception and prejudice concerning alcoholism. He usually has as much contempt for the "drunken bum" as anyone else, and blames that "bum" just as heartily for the condition "he has got himself in." This leads the alcoholic, naturally, to separate himself from the stigma he attaches to such a condition, to consider himself "different" and to seek the cause of his trouble somewhere else than in his drinking. This detour off the main road leading to recognition of his illness is also taken by those around him; it is the result of the *mental climate* in which they all live. The alcoholic needs help to stay on the main road; he needs an atmosphere of knowledge and understanding, which recognizes and accepts alcoholism as a disease like any other, so that he need not be shamed beyond endurance by admitting that he may have it. He should be able to recognize the nature of his ailment without shame—and to seek help without shame. This depends almost entirely on the *mental climate* surrounding him.

Equally important to the alcoholic is the mental climate in which he attempts his recovery. If it is one of contempt for his "weakness," it may well lead to ridicule of his efforts not to drink. "Come on, be a man! Have one or two and then stop" is a phrase which has been heard far too often by struggling alcoholics. Or "What's the matter with you—scared? Just one won't hurt you," is another far too frequent taunt. Even more dangerous is the skeptical observer who obviously does not believe the alcoholic can do it, and whose remarks to that effect inevitably get back to the alcoholic. The skeptic is not deliberately harmful; he has simply lived too long in a mental climate composed of belief in a variety of old saws. Typical of these is the one mentioned above: "Once a drunk, always a drunk."

Actually, this particular old saw never did have any truth in it. There have always been alcoholics who recovered, who took up again, after their temporary eclipse, all of the responsibilities and activities that belong to adult life, sometimes carrying more than their share. Every schoolboy has read the story of one of these: General Sam Houston, famous in American history. Houston was already an outstanding personality in his native Tennessee when he made his mysteriously unfortunate marriage. Romantics will remember how his beautiful young wife left him the day after their wedding; no explanation was ever given, but Houston reacted violently, according to the records. It is not made clear in contemporary accounts how much he drank before this dramatic episode, but extremely heavy drinking was very usual in frontier country in those days, and it is never suggested that Houston had been a teetotaler. In any case it is recorded that he remained drunk for many years, going off to live with an Indian tribe who befriended him. When trouble arose in the territory which is now Texas, a group of his friends decided that Houston was the man needed as a leader, and determined to try and draw him back into the stream of life. They visited him in the Indian encampment where he lived, and it is reported that they found him "sodden with drink," and knew that this was his constant condition. Nevertheless they talked with him, and persuaded him to make an effort to pull himself together. We all know with what results, for General Sam Houston was the successful leader of the Texas War for Independence; became

Governor when Texas was made a state, and remains Texas' most popular hero.

Houston was, of course, a remarkable character, and therefore constitutes an unusual case. In most cases the facts were not known, and could not, therefore, give hope to others. There are numerous historical documents where similar stories can be read between the lines, by a student who is looking for such things (I was myself such a researcher for several years), but they are never clearly told. The trouble was, in the past, that such people were careful *not* to advertise their recovery, or to allude to the illness they had suffered. They did not dare. In the first place it was not regarded as an illness, but as a sign of a weak or degenerate character. In the second place, the old saws were so widely held, and the stigma surrounding alcoholism (called simply, drunkenness) was so heavy and dark that they feared jeopardizing their entire futures. And they were right.

There was a further reason for silence, too. Rarely did they have any idea of just what had brought about their recovery, of just how and when it had occurred, or even how long a duration it would have. So why talk about it? Still another reason was that they were usually alone, isolated from others like themselves; often not knowing that there were others like themselves. As a result of this silence, recovery from alcoholism was not generally believed in until very recently.

Belief in the possibility of recovery is growing apace today, but it had a slow and feeble beginning not so very long ago. In the years just following the first World

War, word got around in certain circles (mostly wealthy) that a man named Courtenay Baylor in Boston was having some success in treating alcoholics. He was not a doctor, or a formally trained psychologist: he was what is called a lay therapist, and he worked in a clinic which was part of Emmanuel Church, the seat of the Emmanuel Movement. The methods he used were both psychological and spiritual, combining to re-educate the alcoholic to a life without alcohol; he described them fully in his book *Remaking a Man*, published in 1919. The Emmanuel clinic was for all kinds of nervous disorders, and did not specialize in alcoholism, so that there was no great flood of recoveries to startle the world. Nevertheless a little hope was generated, and some alcoholics got well. A start had been made.

Richard Peabody, also of Boston, was the next name to be associated with recoveries from alcoholism. Himself a product of Baylor's teaching, he turned what he had learned wholly onto the problem of alcoholism, and specialized in the treatment of alcoholics. His book *The Common Sense of Drinking*, containing a description of his method, was published in 1931. A few of his successful cases entered the field as therapists, and by the mid-'thirties still more recoveries were giving the lie to the alleged "hopelessness of alcoholism."

Francis T. Chambers, Jr., of Philadelphia, was a follower of Peabody, who, in turn, went a step further than his teacher. Under the guidance of Dr. Edward A. Strecker, one of America's leading psychiatrists, Chambers took some formal training at the University of Pennsylvania Medical School, and entered the Institute of Pennsylvania Hospital, as Associate Therapist, specializing in alcoholism, but working in conjunction with a team of medically trained personnel. *Alcohol, One Man's Meat*, published in 1938, is the book written jointly by Strecker and Chambers about their work. Out of their hands has flowed a small but steady stream of recoveries ever since.

The methods of all of the above have been generally lumped together under the heading of "lay therapy," a type of treatment which has had considerable success. One of its greatest contributions, however, was the proof it furnished that alcoholics could recover. This fact was a stimulus to other workers and researchers, and helped provide a nucleus of favorable opinion to experimenters with other methods. Most important of all, word began to reach alcoholics that there was not only a name for what ailed them—"alcoholism"—but hope that they might recover.

The farm established in Rhode Island in the mid-'thirties by Charles Durfee, Ph.D., and his wife, a clinical psychologist, also taught re-education to a life without alcohol, using geographical change and outdoor work as therapeutic aids. Durfee's book *To Drink or Not to Drink* was published in 1938. Some recoveries from there added to the growing roll.

At the same time, out on the West Coast, an entirely different approach was being tried, a method based on Pavlov's famous conditioned reflex experiments with dogs. The Shadel Sanitarium, first in Seattle, later also in Portland, Oregon, was giving alcoholics a medical treatment designed to produce a conditioned reflex against alcohol. The idea was an ancient one, but the method was new, worked out on a modern scientific basis. Carefully screening would-be patients, they achieved a high percentage of recoveries among those accepted, and in the Northwest section of the country particularly, word began to spread that alcoholics *could* recover.

Further impetus was given to this new development by the Oxford Group, a religious movement which encouraged its members to make public testimonials. Several alcoholics, who had stopped drinking through the spiritual "change" advocated by the Oxford Group, became prominent speakers and spread their stories widely. One, Charles Clapp, wrote a book on his experiences as an alcoholic called *The Big Bender*. All this helped further to demolish the ancient misbelief that all alcoholics were hopeless propositions.

Little by little gains were being made all through the 'thirties. People, here and there, were recovering from alcoholism; perhaps not in great numbers, but enough to show that it could be done. Cases helped by doctors, psychiatrists, analysts, or the treatment provided at one of the good sanitariums, continued to swell the over-all number. But it remained a scattered number of individuals (an unknown number at that) and not a group of people. They rarely knew one another, had no opportunities of meeting. There was no way for them to gain, from association with one another, the strength and confidence so often needed for the long run, and knowledge that the others were still there, and still sober.

Not until the formation of Alcoholics Anonymous, in 1935, did these things become possible. Here, for the first time, was an idea based on a group of alcoholics helping one another, presenting a united front to an un-sympathetic world, sharing their problems and experi-ences, and gaining strength from one another. And here also, for the first time, was a vital reason for talking about their own recoveries. If they were to help other alcoholics, they had to find them, so the facts about their own recoveries had to be made known, not only to other alcoholics, but to people who might lead them to other alcoholics, or rather send other alcoholics to them for help. Further, they felt they knew exactly how they had recovered, and that they could pass this knowledge on to those who needed it. Their phenomenal success would seem to prove that they were right in this—but it also proves that the message of hope their own talked-about recoveries carried to alcoholics everywhere was most desperately needed and eagerly welcomed. Starting with two men in June, 1935, Alcoholics Anonymous, by 1957, had approximately two hundred thousand men and women, recovered alcoholics, in its membership.

Today this is the greatest single proof we have that alcoholics can recover. It should give the lie forever to the old saws. It should make the new mental climate a necessity for all thinking people, and this in turn can make recoveries possible on a hitherto undreamt-of scale.

8

THE ROAD TO RECOVERY

It is quite possible, now, to make a map showing the road to recovery. In point of fact, such a map would show many roads leading to that happy destination. Not all of them are straight or direct; some go just a short distance, leading into another road, but all of them can carry the alcoholic toward recovery if he will put his foot to the path. If he is not yet ready or willing to do this, there are also roads for families and friends to take, which may help the alcoholic to become ready and willing.

It might be helpful to go over one of the routes now available. It is a route which may appear long and circuitous to a desperately impatient wife—or husband —of an active alcoholic, but sometimes, it is well to remember, "the longest way round" may be "the shortest way home." And always one has to take the first steps on a journey to anywhere.

Young Mrs. David E. was more than ready to take those first steps when she read an article in the newspaper describing a new service in her community. It had a startling name: the Alcoholism Information and Consultation Center. According to the paper, this was an office where anyone could go for information about the disease of alcoholism. She read the last phrase over several times, for while she had been tentatively trying out the word alcoholism in her mind for some time, she had never thought of it as a disease. She looked carefully at the address: it was one of the big business buildings downtown—nothing to be afraid of. She had to be careful, for no one knew of her growing concern over Dave except Dave himself.

They had had their hundredth scene last night, and in the course of it he had wakened the children and badly frightened them. They did not recognize as their normally quiet and gentle father this loud, rough, red-faced and dishevelled man who had shaken them from their sleep in a violent display of what was meant to be affection. Thank God they were so young—at two and a half and five children forget quickly. But she must not allow it to happen again. She had threatened to take the children and leave. And yet this morning, when he lay shaking on the bed, unable to get up and shave, she had once again phoned his office and told the old tale of his chronic "stomach ailment." She could practically see the disbelief on Mr. Morris's face as he expressed his regret and told her to "take good care of Dave." There was something she didn't like about the tone in which he had insisted that she keep Dave home "long enough to really get over it this time." She felt exposed in her lie—the lie she had told so often during this past year. Now Dave was asleep, and she had combed the house high and low without finding any more bottles to dispose of. Mary E. was long past the period of bringing him a stiff drink to help him get his feet to the ground and his clothes on. She hoped he couldn't get out of bed for the rest of the day.

An hour later she opened the door with its neat lettering "Alcoholism Information and Consultation Center of the X Committee on Alcoholism." A friendly-looking woman in her forties was on the phone, but gave a cheerful nod and a welcoming wave of her hand to Mary, who glanced quickly around the pleasant room. Nicer than a doctor's waiting room, she decided, and her eye fixed on a long table covered with pamphlets. Two people were seated in comfortable chairs: a gray-haired woman immersed in a pamphlet, and a youngish man, nicely dressed but with an unnatural pallor and beads of sweat glistening on his forehead. He was staring straight ahead with his hands dangling between his knees, apparently oblivious to his surroundings. The woman behind the desk hung up the phone and beckoned to Mary, who suddenly wished she were a thousand miles away. But the others didn't seem to be noticing her, and somehow she managed to speak: she wanted information about alcoholism. "For an article perhaps?" asked the friendly woman, and Mary almost seized upon this, but her need was too desperate. "No," she stammered, "it's my husband . . ." Before she could go on, the woman was looking at an appointment pad. "You'll want to see Mrs. Dick. She has someone with her now, and that young man is next. But he won't be long—he's on his way to the hospital. If you could wait ten or fifteen minutes, I could give you something to read—something that will help you. If you can't wait, we can make an appointment——" Mary interrupted. "I'll wait."

So she settled down on the couch with a pamphlet "Do's and Don'ts for Wives" and a little descriptive folder about the Center and its services. So absorbed did she become with the words that seemed to be shedding a bright light on the darkest corners of her fears that she jumped when the friendly woman touched her shoulder. The little office she entered seemed to wrap her in warmth. The face which greeted her was open and welcoming, and alive with understanding. Mary's story poured out in a flood.

Half an hour later she left with her head high and hope shining in her eyes. Under her arm was a big envelope filled with literature. In her mind were the clear outlines of a plan worked out with Mrs. Dick. She knew now it would take time to help Dave, and that at this point it all depended on her. But at last she knew what she was dealing with, she had tools to use, and a counselor to advise and encourage her. She had another appointment with Mrs. Dick in two weeks' time.

Mary did not find the going easy. All too often she reverted to her old pattern, when Dave drank too much. She wept and pleaded, scolded and threatened. But she managed to believe in her new insights and to follow the plan often enough to clearly see the difference in Dave's reactions, and so to be convinced that this new approach would work someday. She was treating Dave like the very sick man he was, but with very firm tactics. She leaned heavily on Mrs. Dick in her times of discouragement, and to her own amazement realized one day that she was learning many things about herself from these sessions. On one memorable occasion she confessed that she was coming to feel she had as many faults as Dave, and needed help just as badly. Mrs. Dick smiled and told her she wasn't alone, that most wives of alcoholics discovered the same thing, and wouldn't she like to meet some of these "fellow sufferers"? Mary hesitated, for she had never moved far out of her own sheltered middle-class circles, and she wondered . . . "You know," said Mrs. Dick gently, "you already know such a woman. Mrs. Jennings, at the desk outside, is the wife of an alcoholic. Her husband is recovered and is an active member of Alcoholics Anonymous. She is equally active in an Alanon Family Group. She'll take you along if you'd like to go to one of their meetings."

Mary went, and for the first time found women, and a few men, who understood more about her problems than she did herself. Her feeling of confidence in the future grew apace as she realized that, indeed, she wasn't alone; that there was real support here, and understanding and friendship. She learned the principles of A.A., and that she could apply them to help herself, and she learned what A.A. could and could not do for Dave. It could not do anything at this point, for Dave had still not admitted that he needed any help.

It was a little over seven months from Mary's first visit to the Information Center when the day finally came. Dave had returned in the early hours of the morning from a three-day bender—the first time he had ever stayed away all night. Mary felt she was still alive and functioning only because of her Alanon friends, who had rallied to her side and given her the enormous comfort of sharing their own similar experiences. Their advice had kept her from tearing all over town seeking Dave, or from calling the police, or from any other overt moves. Although Dave was still missing on Monday, she hadn't even called his office. Now it was Tuesday morning.

Dave was sick, desperately sick, and he knew it. For the first time he begged Mary to "do something—help me—get a doctor—anything, I'll do anything." Mary moved into the second phase of the plan. She called Mrs. Dick, who made the necessary arrangements. She called two of her Alanon friends, whose A.A. husbands showed up at the noon hour to help get Dave dressed and into the car. By one o'clock he was ensconced in a private room in one of the city's best general hospitals. By two o'clock the doctor had finished his examination, the medication had done its work, and Dave was sleeping peacefully.

When Dave was wakened at dinnertime, he was sober and hungry. Afterwards Mary felt it was time to talk, and found Dave receptive. She outlined the next steps: three to five days in the hospital, depending on the doctor's orders. Then a visit to the Alcoholism Information Center or, if he preferred, first to the doctor's office for further treatment. Either the doctor or Mrs. Dick would take it from there, but Mary explained to Dave that this was a long-term proposition. He would need some kind of treatment for a long time to come, for he was fighting a deadly serious disease. She would be with him all the way, for she had learned about it now and knew what to do. And she told him that she loved him, and wanted only to help him get well. Dave was overwhelmed, with remorse, with gratitude, and with a great deal of self-pity. He clung to Mary, and she tried to share her hope with him.

Dave visited the doctor's office regularly for several weeks. He was given vitamin shots, and a carefully counted small supply of a tranquilizing drug. He was feeling fine. The doctor talked to him of A.A., but Dave was resistant. He felt sure he could manage without "that last resort," and besides he preferred a more orthodox and formalized treatment. He was willing to take treatment, but he wanted to choose *which* treatment. The doctor acquiesced and made an appointment for Dave with Mrs. Dick. He liked her, and saw her several times. She recognized that he wished to become her patient, but this she could not allow, for her function was not to give treatment, but to persuade him to take it, and then to make the best possible referral. She had to keep her time free for the constant stream of new cases that poured into the Center and for the educational and other work that made up the Center's varied functions. And so she consulted the doctor and together they worked out the best plan for Dave: a visit to a psychiatrist who specialized in alcoholism, and who conducted several group therapy sessions for alcoholics, in the evenings.

Very reluctantly Dave visited the psychiatrist for an initial interview, and promptly got drunk. Several days later he turned up at the doctor's office, considerably shaken and asking for more tranquilizers. Instead, the doctor suggested Antabuse. He told Dave this "chemical fence" would protect him from unintended drinking, and explained its action in detail. He emphasized that this alone would not be enough for Dave, that it would merely enable him to stay sober while he underwent treatment—whatever treatment Dave chose. Once again the doctor urged consideration of A.A. And once again Dave resisted. He preferred the psychiatrist.

For the next six months Dave took his Antabuse regularly, went to his group therapy session every Tuesday, saw the psychiatrist alone very occasionally. Mary saw a steady difference in him. He was less tense, less irritable; he was slowly becoming comfortable in his sobriety. And he was beginning to want to talk about the whole thing. Mary was now deep in her Alanon group—she went to her meeting the night he went to group therapy. They began to exchange anecdotes and to compare notes, and then they began to exchange books. Soon they were talking happily far into the night about "their" subject.

One night Dave remarked quite casually that he'd like to go to one of her meetings, and Mary told him they were having a joint meeting with A.A. in a few weeks at which he would be more than welcome. He was a little shy on entering the room, but almost immediately was warmly greeted by a man and a woman Mary did not know. He proudly introduced her, and she learned they were members of his therapy group, and also members of A.A. At the coffee hour after the meeting (which Dave had followed with intense interest), the man invited them both to dinner and an open A.A. meeting the following week. Mary waited, and smiled happily when Dave accepted with enthusiasm.

That was the beginning. Very soon Dave was regularly attending A.A. meetings as well as his group-therapy sessions, and they were going together to open meetings. After a few months Dave announced he had completed his group therapy, but on Tuesdays he would now attend a closed A.A. meeting. Mary relaxed completely, for she felt that Mrs. Dick's plan was now accomplished.

And so their life moved forward, busy, happy, useful. Sometimes Mary wondered how she could ever repay Mrs. Dick, Mrs. Jennings, and the Alcoholism Information Center for the great gift she had received. She made an annual contribution to the Committee on Alcoholism, which maintained the Center and its free services, but it seemed to her a very inadequate return. Finally she asked Mrs. Jennings, and found there was volunteer work she could do at the time of their Annual Meeting. She began to learn more of the committee and its total community program; of the need for wider understanding of its work, and for more adequate support; of the committee's plan for an out-patient clinic where payment for treatment such as Dave had had would be on a sliding scale, or free if necessary, and where all types of treatment would be available in one spot. Most of all Mary learned of the need to keep fighting the old stigma that still keeps so many alcoholics hidden, and of how the committee used every weapon of modern communication in this fight. Dave was in advertising; perhaps he could be helpful here. Mary joined the committee, and later became a member of its board. Gradually Dave became interested, and offered to serve on its subcommittee on public relations. Mary and Dave were repaying their debt, not just to the committee, but to society for the helping hand it had extended to them in their hour of desperate need. And they both knew that every contribution they made, in time, in money, in energy and in brain power, was helping to build a wider, smoother road down which more alcoholics could walk to recovery.

Here then is one route which is currently leading many hundreds of alcoholics to the destination of a healthy, happy, productive life. It is compounded of not one, but many roads, each leading the sufferer—and his family—a little further toward the goal. Each bit of road is important in the total journey; without any one of them the alcoholic, or the family, might lose their way in the wilderness of alcoholism, might be trapped there.

Not everyone uses, or needs to use, this identical route. Many people achieve recovery by traversing just one, or two, of the roads mentioned. For this reason we will give some attention to each of the roads in the following chapters.

9

ALCOHOLISM INFORMATION CENTERS[1]

This is the most advanced outpost in the fight against alcoholism. It is much farther out than the front-line troops of therapists, hospitals, clinics and Alcoholics Anonymous. It is the headquarters of a special task force, the local Committee on Alcoholism, which must penetrate deep into hostile territory, infiltrating through combat lines of prejudice, to establish this bridgehead of hope for the captive people behind those lines: alcoholics and their families.

The Alcoholism Information and Consultation Center is not in itself the road to recovery. It is actually a bridge leading to that road, and a very necessary bridge. The bulk of our alcoholic population is still hidden, still sealed off from help by an impassable swamp: a No Man's

---

[1] To find your nearest Alcoholism Information Center, consult your telephone directory, or write to: The National Council on Alcoholism, 2 East 103 Street, New York 29, New York.

Land of ignorance, fear, superstition and stigma. This swamp is a black morass, with an unpleasant stench of contempt and hostility rising from it. It is a fearsome thing, and the average alcoholic in the early or middle stages of his illness, is quite unable to face it, much less to conquer it. His family is no more able to than he. If they are to find the way out of their dilemma, they must be reached, and a way provided across the swamp: a bridge that will lift them right over it. This is the function of the Alcoholism Information Center.

The Center works two ways to provide this bridge: (1) education (alcohol*ism*) and (2) services (alcohol*ics*).

Education--Alcoholism

The primary task is to reach the people in need, with the information they must have to survive. This requires a broad over-all educational program. It must be designed to reach directly the general public (among whom alcoholics and their families are hidden), and to stimulate special groups to interest and action.

These special groups offer a key to public attitudes. They include clergymen, doctors, lawyers, judges, management, labor, health and welfare workers, teachers and all kinds of clubs and associations. Put together they make up the influential world of public opinion, the original though unintentional creators of the swampy morass described above, and, therefore, the only ones who can eventually drain it and make it safe for human passage. Education will one day accomplish this, but by its nature it is a long slow process, and it must always begin with the general before it can progress to the specific. The Information Center, therefore, gives priority to an intensive and continuing educational campaign, using the press, radio, TV, films; setting up a Speaker's Bureau; conducting seminars, workshops, conferences; putting on public meetings, institutes and forums; in short, utilizing every method of communication to bring the facts to the attention of the public.

Experience has shown that, as these facts percolate into the public consciousness, both individuals and groups come forward in increasing numbers, seeking specific information and assistance. Teachers, students, journalists and authors request background material and advice. Others want simply "information" or "something to read." Clubs request materials for a program. Not least of the Information Center's educational services is the distribution of literature. Each Center also maintains a library, stocking many of its books for sale. In addition there is a wide variety of pamphlets, free for the asking. The Centers are supplied by their own national headquarters, the National Council on Alcoholism, which publishes and distributes over seventy different pamphlets, covering eleven separate categories. There is something for everyone in this wide range of materials.

Before the Information Center can give the services included under the heading "alcohol*ics*," it must discover the existing resources in the community. This is actually the job of the Committee itself, that dedicated group of representative citizens who established, and who maintain, the Information Center as a service to their community. A survey usually uncovers more resources than anyone had suspected. There are always a few doctors who have been quietly caring for alcoholics, and somehow finding hospital beds for them when necessary; always some clergymen who have been making special efforts to help alcoholics. Many public and private agencies (health and welfare departments, Salvation Army and Volunteers of America, family and children's agencies, mental-health clinics, state mental hospitals, etc.) have been patiently struggling, usually separately and alone, to deal with alcoholism in addition to their other work. And always, everywhere, Alcoholics Anonymous has been functioning as a major resource.

Having discovered all possible resources, the Information Center becomes a co-ordinating point for their best utilization. It may bring the special knowledges and skills of several of these resources to bear upon a single case. It notes the gaps in available services and attempts to stimulate new resources to fill those gaps. Again, this is the work of the Committee itself, through its various subcommittees, but all this effort is channeled through the Center as Committee headquarters. The Center, therefore, is a mine of information as well as a specific source of help.

Finally, the Information Center Director works to alert the personnel of other agencies and facilities, and the personnel departments of business and industry, in order that they may help uncover hidden cases and direct them to a source of help. Every avenue is used to accelerate the flow of needed information. The goal is to secure a better application, by more and more people, of our existing knowledge.

Services--Alcoholism

This heading implies services to alcoholics themselves, if and when they come personally to the Center, or telephone there, for information and/or guidance. And they do come, more and more of them as the educational program reduces their fears and their resistance. But it also implies services to nonalcoholics about their alcoholic. One Center in its reports, divides the people who use these services into two groups: (1) patients—alcoholics themselves, and (2) clients—families, friends, employers and anyone else who calls or comes in about a particular alcoholic.

The previous chapter has shown in considerable detail what can happen in both instances. Mary E.—a client—came first, and the Center personnel helped and guided her over many months before her husband, Dave —a patient—could be brought there. Both client and patient were given information and consultation at the Center. Both were referred to other resources for help. In Dave's case several resources were brought into play. But this was an above-average-income family, and Dave still had his job. All cases at an Information Center are not in this category, and may require referral to different resources.

Victor S. was an expert mechanic, but he had not worked at it for many months. He existed by an occasional night job washing cars. His sister, an office secretary with no funds to care for Vic, came to the Center first. She had heard a radio program which told of the free services offered by the Alcoholism Information and Consultation Center, and she requested a private interview with the Director. She had several interviews before she was able to lead Vic in. He was in shocking physical condition and utterly broke, yet he was strongly resisting his sister's pleas that he "go away for a while." The Director of this Center was a man, highly trained and able. It took him only twenty minutes alone with Vic to win his agreement, and arrangements were immediately made with a house run by a devoted priest for just such alcoholic cases. A volunteer was recruited to drive Vic to this sanctuary where he remained for several months, working for his keep as soon as he was physically restored. There he learned of A.A. and began to attend meetings. When he returned to the city, the Center helped him regain a job he had held several times before as chief mechanic for a fleet of Salvation Army trucks. This gave him room and board. Vic stuck to A.A. and gradually made his way back to a good job in a big garage, and a home of his own, which he shares with his sister.

Gladys D. was referred to the Alcoholism Information Center in her city by the Family Service Agency. A spinster, nearing sixty, she had been a telephone operator all her adult life, living alone and friendless outside her working day. Her increasingly "queer" behavior had caused her supervisor to send her to the company medical department, and they had referred her to the agency. But the agency social worker was getting nowhere, and finally consulted the Center. When Gladys appeared, she flatly denied that she drank at all, but she liked the woman in charge and wanted to come back. It took several interviews to extract an admission of her drinking, and then the dam broke and she told all. Product of a strict Protestant upbringing, she considered herself bad beyond telling—a lost soul. The disease concept had never entered her head, and she listened with amazement to the description of the city's alcoholism clinic, located in a hospital, and just for people like her.

The next day she went to the clinic for a complete physical and psychiatric examination and, after several private interviews, was admitted to one of the group-therapy sessions. Despite a few rocky periods, Gladys did well in the group, and as she began to come out of her shell, she made friends and her horizons broadened. She continued meeting with the group for over a year, and since that ended, has dropped in on her friends at the Center several times. She has become very active in her church, and looks forward to her imminent retirement with anticipation and confidence.

There are hundreds and hundreds of real-life illustrations of the very special role played by this bridge between hidden alcoholics and the help that is waiting for them. It reaches them, and they will come to it, just *because* it is not itself a method of treatment, or a treatment center. It is neutral ground to them, and they will risk treading on it. They can go and ask for information (often stating it is "for a friend"), and they can go away. No noose has slipped down over their necks, no commitment has been asked for or given. They are not even identified by going there, since others in the waiting room may include a high-school student poring over a book, a Committee member there on business, a clergy-man getting a supply of pamphlets for his church rack, or a woman whose club is working on alcoholism as a project. Alcoholics, like others, are taken at their word as to why they are there, and given what they ask for, often including an interpretation or explanation of various forms of treatment. For this is a bridge *leading* to the road to recovery—it is not that road. Yet, in the great majority of cases it leads the alcoholics who come there to help—and to health and happiness as well.

10

TREATMENT

The Acute Phase

Alcoholism, like most other diseases, has two phases: acute and chronic. For the purpose of treatment, this division is highly important, because it clarifies an old misunderstanding, still held by those hospital administrators, staffs, and nurses who maintain that "general hospitals have no place for the treatment of alcoholism." In a sense they are right, but it is the wrong sense. General hospitals are ideally suited for the short-term treatment of *acute* alcoholism. On the other hand, the *chronic* condition rarely requires hospitalization, and is better handled on an out-patient basis. The treatment of acute alcoholism is primarily a medical problem. The treatment of the chronic condition, the alcoholism itself, must remain, in the present state of our knowledge, largely psychological: the re-education of the alcoholic to a life without drinking. This is a long-term proposition.

The acute phase means an alcoholic in a state of

extreme intoxication, whether of recent origin or of long duration. It may also mean an alcoholic who has apparently sobered up, probably by himself, but is showing acute physical symptoms such as dehydration, extreme nervousness, sleeplessness, tremors, and general physical discomfort, all recognized today as part of the "withdrawal symptoms" of alcoholic drinking. In either case the alcoholic needs medical care, and frequently hospital care. In some cases the latter is essential. This condition is not for the psychiatrist, the psychologist, or the social worker; nor is it for the lay member of Alcoholics Anonymous to handle. It requires the attention of a skilled medical practitioner, and sometimes the additional skills of a trained nurse. Laboratory and other special equipment which is available only in a hospital may have to be brought into play. The acute phase of alcoholism can be extremely dangerous, for there can be serious complications.

Few alcoholics—or their families—seem to realize this. They are reluctant to call the doctor, or even to go to the doctor's office. Part of this reluctance can, unhappily, be traced to the even greater reluctance of many doctors to answer such calls, or to accept such patients. Fortunately their number is dwindling, and American medicine itself, through its own organization, the American Medical Association, is calling for a new look at alcoholism as a major medical responsibility. More and more physicians are learning to use the information which is being made available to them in their own professional journals; and the newer drugs have made their task relatively easy, particularly where hospital beds are available.

The use of the newer drugs "has all but revolutionized the treatment of the acute alcoholic stage," according to Dr. Marvin Block,[1] Chairman of the Committee on Alcoholism of AMA's Council on Mental Health, for their action is so swift that even the most severely intoxicated patient no longer presents a behavior problem in the hospital or at home. Chief among these medications are the group known as the "tranquilizing drugs," all of which give the patient a sense of relaxation and comfort, which induces sleep. Four of these drugs are currently in wide use: their technical names are reserpine, chlorpromazine, promazine hydrochloride, meprobamate.

Reserpine is the slowest acting, but its effect seems to last longer. Its trade name is Serpasil, and it is derived from *Rauwolfia serpentina*, which has been used in India for hundreds of years to calm the agitated. Because of its slower action it is not as popular as the other tranquilizers, but it has a valued place nonetheless.

Chlorpromazine, known as Thorazine, was the first of these drugs to be tested on alcoholics in the acute stage, and the results caused a near sensation. The drug increases the sedative action of the alcohol itself (which, of course, is chemically an anesthetic, although the world refuses to accept this scientific fact), so that no other sedation is required. This was great news, indeed, for

[1] "Medical Treatment of Alcoholism," by Marvin A. Block, M.D. *Journal of the American Medical Association*, December 29, 1956.

specialists in this field of medicine had long been deeply concerned over the dangers of giving sedatives to alcoholics. Sedatives, particularly the barbiturates (Seconal, Nembutal, sodium amytal, etc.) are habituating. Alcoholics are already habituated to alcohol. And while we do not know the mechanisms of habituation, or addiction, it has been repeatedly observed that an individual addicted to one drug (and alcohol is a drug, albeit a "domesticated drug" in universal use, and so not thought of in those terms), can apparently make an easy switch to another drug. Too many alcoholics become "pill-takers" to doubt this fact, and the problem of barbiturate addiction concurrent with or following on alcoholism is a very serious one. Chlorpromazine, therefore, offered enormous advantages, although, like most drugs, it had some disadvantages, too.

Promazine hydrochloride was developed from chlorpromazine, and has shed some of its predecessor's disadvantages. Known as Sparine, it is particularly valuable with the acutely disturbed alcoholic because of its quick action and the tranquil sleep it brings. At this writing its use is still under study.

Finally we come to meprobamate, known to all who can see, hear and read as Miltown (or Equanil). This is the one drug among the invaluable tranquilizers which has raised serious questions, for it has been accused of causing habituation in much the same way as the barbiturates. The argument rages pro and con, and probably will for a long time to come. Meanwhile it is the most widely used of all the tranquilizers, and not by any means for alcoholism alone, or just by alcoholics. Properly prescribed *by a qualified physician*, who knows enough about alcoholics to give only very small quantities at a time, it has enormous value. This value lies in reducing tension and producing relaxation without sleep. Meprobamate, therefore, is more frequently used to carry the jittery alcoholic *after* the initial medical treatment or hospitalization, and therein, of course, lies its danger as well as its value. It may well be a two-edged sword just as the barbiturates are, but we need swords in this battle provided we handle them carefully.

All the tranquilizing drugs have some beneficial effect, but perhaps the most important is their substitution for the proven dangers of the older drugs such as barbiturates and bromides, paraldehyde, Demerol, and chloral hydrate, all of which have taken a heavy toll among alcoholics with their peculiar susceptibility to habituation. The newer drugs have an added value that none of the older drugs had. They relieve nausea and stop vomiting, allowing the very sick alcoholic to sleep peacefully, and awake refreshed and with a good appetite. Since most alcoholics, after long drinking, suffer from severe dietary deficiency, in fact, from starvation, eating is most important to their recovery, and the sooner they can begin to eat properly the better.

Equally important is the effect the tranquilizing drugs have had upon hospital policies. There is no longer reason to fear the "disturbing influence" of the alcoholic patient. He requires no more care than the patient coming down from the operating room, and he recovers much more quickly. He is often the most co-operative patient in the hospital, and helpful, too; for he soon feels well enough to move around and make himself useful, and he likes doing it. Hospitals are reflecting this change, just as the medical profession is, and the family can now be reasonably assured of getting the best of care for their alcoholic if they seek it.

And they should seek it, for while such treatment is by no means a "cure" for alcoholism, it has great value in preparing the alcoholic both mentally and physically to undertake further treatment, and to understand and adopt some program of recovery. It hardly needs saying that while he is drinking he is not in any condition to plan his future. For one thing, he is still too dependent on alcohol's making him feel well enough to function to consider doing without it. For another, he cannot think straight with alcohol in his system. One of the great functions of good medical care is to get the alcohol quickly out of his system and make him feel well without it. This permits him to reason again, and if, at the same time, the physician can explain the nature of his illness to him, and help him to accept it for what it is—a progressive and deadly disease that requires a serious and consistent effort on his part if it is to be treated successfully—then the alcoholic has a good start toward eventual recovery.

Experience has shown that an excellent time to make such a start is during the acute phase—in the hangover period to be precise. The alcoholic's brain has cleared somewhat, his defenses are down, and he is willing and able to listen. Also he is beginning to feel that he will live after all, and to wonder just how. Many doctors strongly recommend a follow-up program at this juncture, such as psychiatric and clinical treatment, Alcoholics

Anonymous, or both. This has tremendous value coming from a physician, for alcoholics will often listen to their doctor far more readily than anyone else.

It is at this juncture, too, that Disulfiram, commonly known as Antabuse, is likely to be recommended as a "shield" against drinking while long-term treatment is being undertaken. Antabuse has been much misunderstood, largely because the average layman considers it a treatment in itself. It is not. It is merely a "chemical fence," which prevents the alcoholic from drinking while undergoing treatment. Antabuse is a drug which has no effect unless alcohol is added. A nondrinker could take Antabuse every day with no more effect than if he took sugar pellets. But with Antabuse in the system, a man cannot swallow a single drink without a violent and very uncomfortable reaction. Dr. Block has described it in detail:

> Within a few minutes of alcoholic ingestion, there is a flushing of the face that extends down over the neck and chest and becomes deeper and deeper until the skin is bright red. There is a sensation of great heat in the area, followed by a pounding headache that becomes very severe. The blood pressure rises suddenly with this headache, but within a few minutes there occurs a precipitous drop in the blood pressure, giving the patient and sense of faintness and nausea, sometimes followed by violent vomiting.[2]

It is obvious that such a drug cannot be given to a patient without his full knowledge and consent. It is necessary to fully explain to the alcoholic what Antabuse

---

[2] Block, *ibid.*

will do, both positively and negatively. It can do much in giving him support while he takes the long road to recovery. It completely blocks all impulsive drinking, so he literally cannot "take one without thinking" or "without realizing what he is doing." He has to make only *one* decision a day, when he takes his tablet, so that he is relieved of his preoccupation with drinking, of the day-long refrain "to drink or not to drink." He is thus given comparative freedom from his old compulsion to drink, freedom to concentrate on a new way of life without alcohol. Even the negative aspects are helpful to the alcoholic. If he has any doubts as to the efficacy of the drug, the consumption of a very small amount of alcohol will convince him of the serious consequences. He is also given a card, and warned to carry it at all times. It names him and his doctor, and states that he is taking Antabuse and that no alcohol should be administered if he should be found unconscious. This procedure is usually sufficient to convince the alcoholic that he dare not drink.

All this sounds so easy to some alcoholics that they think Antabuse is all they need. This is very far from the truth. Alcoholism is a complex disease, and a period of nondrinking, however long, is not the whole answer. It is too easy to stop taking the drug and thus remove the "shield." Without deep inner changes, such drug-induced sobriety is likely to be very precarious, too easily lost under the stresses and strains that are part of everyone's daily life. Successful treatment of alcoholism itself—the chronic condition—remains psychological in nature and long in time.

The Chronic Phase

The chronic phase of alcoholism really means the alcoholism itself: the condition, whatever its causes, which manifests itself as the *compulsion* to drink regardless of the consequences. This condition is also described as *loss of control* over drinking. No treatment exists which can restore the alcoholic's control so that he may drink normally. This would be a complete "cure"—a word which cannot be used in this field at this stage of our knowledge. The word "recovery" is used instead, and is used in its literal meaning: the recovery of health and well-being; the recovery of sobriety (which after all is the normal state for the nonalcoholic world); the recovery of the ability to live as others do in the everyday world, as a citizen, a parent, a worker, an acceptable member of society; the recovery, in short, of every ordinary human function except one: the ability to drink. This the alcoholic can never do again.

Many treatments exist, however, which are designed to remove the compulsion to drink, or at least to so reduce its force that the alcoholic can live comfortably and happily without drinking at all. These are of necessity psychologically based treatments, since their purpose must be to re-educate the alcoholic to a new life without alcohol. Obviously this life must be a satisfying one *to him*, or he will not want to maintain it. Therefore the treatment must be in depth, must deal with the whole man and his whole life. It cannot hope to succeed if it is merely a surface restriction against drinking, such as Antabuse alone, for instance; or enforced abstinence, however lengthy, through incarceration in an institution, a hospital or jail. It must reach down to the inner man, and help to bring about a change there. Religion has been doing this to people from time immemorial—all kinds of people, not just alcoholics—and it is worth repeating that it has done this to individual alcoholics time and again over the centuries. It can and will continue to do the job for some alcoholics without any other means being employed, and where that is possible it is wonderful, indeed. There are many, however, who are either unable or unwilling to accept the answers which religion offers, and with whom other means of recovery may well succeed. These other means are the subject of this chapter.

Medicine, psychiatry, psychology, social work and nursing—all the modern professional disciplines of the ancient arts of healing—have each contributed something to the treatment of alcoholism. And, of course, alcoholics themselves have contributed their experience, their feelings, their know-how and their desire to help others like themselves, through Alcoholics Anonymous, which will have a chapter to itself. But it is medicine in its broadest sense, including all its specialties and divisions, which has been the means of the tremendous upsurge in treatment facilities in the past few years. All of the disciplines are involved, and in the alcoholism clinic they work together as a team.

There are today enough specialized out-patient clinics for the diagnosis and treatment of alcoholism so that they can be highlighted as a major resource for help for the alcoholic. The National Council on Alcoholism compiles an annual directory of such facilities[1] and they are nationwide and constantly increasing in number. Many of these clinics are supported by tax funds, under the direction of an official state alcoholism program or a municipal health department; some clinics are supported by local voluntary committees on alcoholism; and some are independently run, by hospitals or other interested groups. In all of them the fees are either extremely reasonable and waived if necessary, or there are no fees.

The treatment given varies only slightly. A thorough diagnosis, with a physical, psychiatric and social "work-up" is followed by a recommendation of the particular course to be followed. It will probably include physical care such as vitamin shots, and at least a few interviews with the psychiatrist, and long-term counseling with one particular member of the team: a social worker or perhaps a psychologist. It may also include early introduction into group therapy with this soon becoming the only clinic therapy the patient requires. In most cases the clinic staff urge the alcoholic to attend A.A. meetings as soon as he is willing to do so, while still continuing therapy at the clinic.

Modern treatment, in short, utilizes not only the team approach, but anything else that may offer assistance to the alcoholic in his struggle to regain a sober place in the world. One clinic employs "religious therapists": ministers who have specialized in pastoral counseling, and who work under the medical director as part of the total team.

---

[1] The 1958 edition listed 122 clinics (price 50¢). It may be obtained by writing to the National Council on Alcoholism, 2 East 103 Street, New York 29, New York.

Another clinic uses "art therapy"; still another offers vocational guidance. All methods or approaches that have shown promise of being helpful are in use somewhere, although not all in one clinic, of course. The one method that is in use in every clinic is psychotherapy in some form: individual interviews (whether with psychiatrist, psychologist, social worker or counselor), and/or group therapy under the leadership of any one of the above, or even self-directed with no leader. All of these methods take time, but the effort in the great majority of clinics is to make that time as short as feasible in each case, in order to be able to treat greater numbers of those who need and want help, and of whom there seems to be a never-ending supply.

This is one reason why the entrance of physicians in private practice into this field is so essential. Many general practitioners and internists can give sufficient advice and counseling, while they are treating the physical needs of the alcoholic, to get him started on the road to recovery, either through A.A., or with a private psychiatrist or perhaps with his church. It is important to remember also, that many alcoholics are in the middle- and upper-income brackets, still hold good jobs, and still have what they think of as "a position to keep up." These people often find it extremely difficult, if not impossible, to go to a clinic or to seek help from a group such as Alcoholics Anonymous. In the first instance they are not used to going to "clinics" (unless it is the Mayo Clinic!), but to a specialist in private practice, preferably recommended by their own doctor, who is also a private practitioner. In the second, any group approach is repugnant to them, for many reasons. Such hesitations may be invalid, but are nonetheless very real barriers, which effectively prevent some alcoholics from getting the help they so desperately need.

The psychiatrist in private practice can play a major role in the total attack on alcoholism. He is often the last hope of a despairing family. Yet most alcoholics resist accepting his help as violently as if it were the devil's own powers they were escaping. Why? One reason is simple enough: most adult Americans mistakenly fear that going to a psychiatrist means an admission of mental weakness or abnormality. In alcoholics such fear is redoubled, since they secretly believe this may be exactly true about them. There are other reasons, however, which are more complex.

There seems to be a great deal of general confusion over what constitutes "psychiatric treatment." All too frequently one hears people say, "Oh, yes, he tried psychiatry, and it didn't do him one bit of good." Upon inquiry it turns out that the alcoholic in question visited a psychiatrist once, or at most two or three times. On other occasions one hears, "He had psychiatry in the hospital. It didn't help him." And in these cases it develops that what the alcoholic actually had was one or two visits from a psychiatrist during hospitalization, and that these were interviews for diagnostic purposes, rather than treatment sessions. It is significant that the term generally used is simply the single word "psychiatry," indicating a lack of understanding as to the correct meaning of either the word "psychiatry" or the term "psychiatric treatment," and of what they imply.

The word "psychiatry" is defined in Webster's Dictionary as: "The medical specialty that deals with mental disorders . . . [and] neuroses." "Psychiatric treatment" in turn means specific treatment by a practitioner of that medical specialty. Diagnostic interviews are not treatment: they consist rather of a series of careful questions designed to give the psychiatrist background knowledge of the patient and his problems, so that the psychiatrist may know what is the nature of the patient's illness, whether or not the patient needs treatment, what kind of treatment, and whether or not the patient is likely to respond to treatment. In other words diagnostic interviews must come first, before treatment is begun, and since the diagnosis of an alcoholic frequently requires several interviews, it is unlikely that an alcoholic who has seen a psychiatrist one, two, or even three times has even begun treatment.

Psychiatric diagnosis is valuable in any case of alcoholism or suspected alcoholism. In early cases it can often distinguish between true alcoholism and an underlying mental disorder which requires quite different handling. In later cases it is often the only way of making a sure distinction. In a case of true alcoholism, it can help decide what is the best approach to that case, and what is the type of treatment most likely to succeed. Often the psychiatrist who is making a diagnosis can, in the process, persuade the alcoholic to seek the treatment which is right for him, whether that be medical, psychiatric, clinical, sanitarium care, or Alcoholics Anonymous.

Many alcoholics do not require psychiatric treatment in order to stop drinking. Isolated cases have shown this, and the mass successes of Alcoholics Anonymous would seem to offer conclusive proof. Nevertheless there remain many alcoholics who do need psychiatric treatment before they can succeed in stopping their drinking, and many others who feel that they require this special help after they have stopped, in order to build a sound basis for permanent sobriety. Psychiatric treatment is much more effective when the patient is not drinking. It is difficult, if not impossible, to treat a patient psychiatrically when he is constantly under the influence of liquor, for he cannot think straight nor can he be honest with a psychiatrist. And since psychiatrists do not maintain private detectives, or an intelligence staff, and do not have the "all-seeing eye," in trying to help a patient, they must rely on what that patient tells them. The family, of course, can help in such cases, but even full co-operation from the family is seldom enough without the complete co-operation of the patient. For this reason particularly, most psychiatrists prefer to have their alcoholic patients in a sanitarium while undergoing treatment, at least during the beginning stages of that treatment.

Psychiatric treatment is designed to help the patient gain insight into himself and his behavior, to show him "what makes him tick." He may think, for instance, that "his head rules his heart," only to find under treatment that he has been led around by the nose by his own emotions all his life, without ever knowing it, since he did not understand those emotions, or was not even aware of them. He may think that his only work trouble lies in the personality of his boss, and find through treatment that the trouble lies in the kind of work, and that his temperament and abilities belong in a totally different kind of activity, in which he could be both effective and happy. He may think that he has married the wrong kind of woman, and find, with the doctor's help, that the trouble is an accumulation of small things which can be fairly easily worked out; or he may find that the trouble is, indeed, a fundamental one, and a solution will have to be found which will allow him to live in comparative inner comfort. He may find that his troubles have been entirely created by his way of drinking, and that a cessation of that drinking will, in time, solve them.

The treatment itself consists of conversations between the patient and the doctor, with the patient doing most of the talking, and the doctor rarely doing more than putting careful questions and making suggestions. Psychiatric treatment includes very few direct orders to the patient; it is usually suggested that he "try" this or that method, or possible solution, making his own decisions. In short, the patient brings his problems to the doctor, and together they try to work out a satisfactory solution to them.

Psychoanalysis has been widely confused with psychiatric treatment; actually they are very different methods. To begin with, analysis is a much deeper probing into the patient; it is in fact an effort to look directly into his subconscious mind rather than through his conscious mind. Instead of sitting across a desk in conversation, discussing problems which are on the surface of his mind, the analytic patient lies on a couch with the analyst sitting behind him, out of his sight, and talks in "free association"; that is to say, expresses everything which is going through his mind, whether it seems to make sense, or is connected, or not. Out of this flow of free association come many buried memories and unrecognized emotions, which have been unknown causes of trouble. Other hidden trouble sources are revealed through the patient's dreams, as he describes them to the analyst and tries to translate what the contents mean to him. The process, being deeper and more indirect, is naturally much slower than psychiatric treatment: a complete analysis often takes several years of regular one-hour sessions.

Psychoanalysts will rarely accept alcoholic patients unless they have been sober for a considerable time. The reasons for this are obvious. Free association, which is the main key to the subconscious mind of the patient, cannot be trusted in the case of a patient who is intoxicated most of the time: his thoughts are distorted by his drinking and are not truly revealing. Furthermore, the deep-probing process of analysis can be extremely painful to the patient, and the active alcoholic, in pain, automatically resorts to more alcohol to deaden the pain; so that he is apt to go on binges which are both more prolonged and more severe than before, interrupting and disrupting his regular treatment program. Where an alcoholic has stopped drinking, however, whether by himself or through some other form of treatment, he may find analysis very helpful, particularly if some of his problems seem too deeply rooted and too obscure in their origins to yield to simpler handling, and are not resolved at all by his sobriety.

In many such cases alcoholics who have been sober six months, a year, or more, have resorted to either psychiatric treatment or psychoanalysis for help. Which of the two they chose usually depended on the nature and complexity of their problems. In the words of one doctor, analysis is like a major operation, to be used when no milder measure will work; while psychiatric treatment is like any other medical treatment, to which everyone resorts when unable to handle illness or its results by themselves. The problems which have been created in the life of an alcoholic by years of alcoholism are frequently too difficult and complex to be solved by the same treatment which overcame his alcoholism. He may be the successful product of limited clinical treatment, or a good member of Alcoholics Anonymous, and still be plagued by troubles and inner conflicts which will not yield to simple psychological or even spiritual methods. Such cases derive great benefit from individual psychiatric treatment or analysis.

In recent years an increasing number of psychiatrists have been working in conjunction with Alcoholics Anonymous. When a patient with an alcoholic problem comes to them, they suggest that he try Alcoholics Anonymous, while at the same time undergoing psychiatric treatment. If this works out, it proves helpful in many ways. The A.A. program helps the alcoholic to stop drinking; it helps to fill much of the time he used to spend drinking; in his almost inevitable crisis periods other members are available at any hour; and the program itself awakens him to the nature of many problems he did not know he had. In turn the psychiatrist helps him to understand and use the A.A. program, and assists him in solving many problems, some of which result from his attempt to live without drinking. In some cases psychiatrists suggest Alcoholics Anonymous to a patient, with the further suggestion that he return after a few months' sobriety, if necessary, for psychiatric treatment to supplement A.A. This combination of psychiatry and Alcoholics Anonymous seems to work remarkably well in a great many cases.

The combination is also used in reverse order; that is, where an alcoholic honestly has been trying to stay sober through Alcoholics Anonymous with only partial success, other members may suggest that he try psychiatric treatment as well. Particularly in very difficult cases of neurotic involvement or extremely complex problems, this dual effort has sometimes been successful where either one, taken alone, might have failed. It is a combination which could undoubtedly be enormously helpful in many more cases if psychiatry were more easily available, both geographically and financially.

Future treatment programs should rely heavily on this conjunction of forces, for it has already proved its value. In alcoholic clinics already functioning, or being planned, psychiatric diagnosis and treatment are an important part of their services; of equal importance is the active co-operation of successful members of Alcoholics Anonymous. Each has something to contribute which the other needs, if they are to help more alcoholics more successfully. Working together, they can be expected to return more alcoholics to sober, happy living, *and to keep them there*, than either could do alone. The problem of alcoholism is serious and difficult enough to insist upon the fullest and widest possible use of everything that has ever proved helpful.

There is a less expensive method than individual psychiatric or analytic treatment which is becoming more widely available all the time. Group therapy has been mentioned, and it may be helpful to describe it more fully. It should also be noted that not all group therapy is conducted by clinics—many individual psychiatrists or analysts in private practice conduct group sessions made up of their private patients, and often hold these sessions in the evenings for the benefit of patients who are working. Since the cost of the doctor's time is divided among the group, it follows that this is much less expensive than individual treatment.

Group therapy could be described as a form of psychiatric treatment, since therapy sessions are usually led by a psychiatrist. It is a term, however, which is often loosely used to describe any communal effort at recovery by groups of people, meeting together to discuss and work out their problems, with or without the help of a trained person.

In its medical sense, group therapy is a method of treating a number of people at once. It involves having a group of people, usually with similar problems, meet regularly with a psychiatrist or psychiatrically trained worker, who leads a discussion of those problems. The patients participate in the discussion, frequently bringing up things they wish to discuss or to hear discussed. The leader of the group acts much as a psychiatrist in a private treatment session, in that he poses questions, and makes suggestions, but allows the patients to do most of the talking. His role is to help them understand themselves and their problems, and find possible ways of working out solutions to those problems.

This method has shown itself particularly effective in two respects: it allows more people to be treated at less expense; and it provides a means for patients to help each other, by sharing their problems, and their ideas and efforts at solutions. Since alcoholics have so many problems that are similar, group therapy has been found unusually effective with them.

All the above treatments are predicated on the alcoholic being able to continue living at home and working, while taking his treatment on the same "out-patient" basis that he would use in any condition that required regular visits to the doctor's office. There are cases, however, where this is not feasible. The alcoholic may be too sick, and may require a period of complete rest and care. He may have finally lost his job, one which he valued highly, or his family, whom he truly loved, and be in a state of serious emotional disturbance, needing constant surveillance. His home situation may, for many reasons, be impossible as a setting for recovery. And finally, his distracted family may be in desperate need of a rest from him which will give them all a chance to recover. Many people, therefore, need to know something about places for long-term in-patient care: sanitariums, nursing homes, rest homes, etc.

Unfortunately there is a great need to point out the tremendous variations in treatments given in sanitariums and institutions which say that they "treat alcoholics." This statement is made by many different kinds of places, from small private nursing homes to large and impressive institutions, and includes advertisements of so-called "cures." Let it be said again that *there is no sure "cure" for alcoholism*, and further that there is no quick and easy treatment of it, at any price. There are good and effective treatments, given in well-established and medically approved institutions; there are totally ineffective treatments given in fly-by-night "racket joints"; and there is everything in between.

There are a great many good, medically approved sanitariums in this country. Not all of them accept alcoholics for treatment, but a good many do. Where they take alcoholics, the treatment given is usually psychiatric treatment, with physical therapy, occupational therapy, exercise, and a strictly healthful living regime, to help build up the patient's strength. However, even some of the good sanitariums do not, in the case of alcoholics, put any emphasis on psychiatric treatment, apparently believing that with alcoholics it is enough to build them up physically, and provide them with a disciplined regime to live by. Some quite good sanitariums give their alcoholic patients nothing but custodial care, which amounts to allowing them to live there, in an atmosphere removed from drinking, and from the strains and responsibilities of normal life. Because of these variations even among good places, it is important for families to learn precisely what treatment is given alcoholics, before choosing a sanitarium.

Many places which call themselves sanitariums, are in reality nothing but "health farms." There is nothing to be said against health farms; they do many people a great deal of good; but they rarely help an alcoholic to overcome his alcoholism. It is true that they may put him in excellent physical condition, which in turn may help him to stay away from drinking for a while, but rarely does this have any lasting value. Yet many alcoholics will go to a "health farm" as a "cure," and their own and their families' hopes are alike shattered when they get drunk again.

Other so-called sanitariums are actually nothing but convalescent homes: in other words they do not provide either medical or psychiatric supervision or treatment, although they are sometimes run by a trained nurse, and very occasionally by a (medical) doctor. Again, there is nothing to be said against such places: they perform a very useful function for many people. But they are rarely of much help to an alcoholic, unless he has already stopped drinking and is there to recover his physical health; or unless they work closely with Alcoholics Anonymous, so that its members visit the alcoholic patients, and the patients can attend nearby A.A. meetings. Under these last-named circumstances, some convalescent homes and farms have been able to do a good deal for alcoholic patients.

The types of sanitariums, homes and farms mentioned above are for all kinds of patients: mentally, physically, and/or nervously ill. Alcoholics make up only a part of their "guest lists." The same, of course, is true of state mental hospitals, some of which accept alcoholics. It is very unusual for a state hospital to be able to treat alcoholics, however, even if they can take them in, since all of them are overcrowded and understaffed; and the majority of their patients, serious mental cases, are in even more desperate need than the alcoholics. Such treatment as alcoholics may get in state hospitals depends on the individual hospital, and even more on the doctors on its staff. Most alcoholics committed to state institutions get nothing but custodial care while they are there: they are locked up; they are, therefore, forcibly kept away from drinking (although they can sometimes circumvent even this), so that their physical condition improves. Upon release, however, they usually revert to drinking, for nothing has been done about their alcoholism.

A few state hospitals have made valiant efforts to treat alcoholism: it was in Rockland State Hospital in New York, for instance, that group therapy was first tried with alcoholics, in the mid-'thirties. And it is Central Islip Hospital in New York which more recently has established a special section for alcoholics where they are given treatment. There are numerous exceptions to the general conditions described above, and the exceptions are in many states, from New York, via Indiana and Texas, to California, but it is nonetheless only wise for a family to look into the facilities and to check the treatment provided before committing their alcoholic to a state institution, except as a means of getting him out of harm's way for a while.

A few states with official alcoholism programs have established special hospitals for long-term in-patient care: Connecticut, North Carolina and Florida, for example. In all cases there is a network of out-patient clinics also, which refer patients to the hospital, and to which the patients are referred back for follow-up treatment on discharge from the hospital.

There are private sanitariums and hospitals, too,

which are just for alcoholics. These also vary enormously. Some give just supervision, rest and "a change"; some give good medical care, some have psychiatric treatment available, and some are especially for the purpose of getting the patient interested in Alcoholics Anonymous. They range from good, through mediocre, to bad. The good ones give tried and proven treatments; some of them are closely allied with Alcoholics Anonymous, often being run by A.A. members. And some of the mediocre ones do the same, only not so well. But the bad ones are dangerous, even when they claim a connection with Alcoholics Anonymous, as some of them do.

Most of these last are the aforementioned "racket joints," which advertise "cures" for alcoholism. Some of them have flourished for years, nourished and fed by the stigma surrounding alcoholism, and the fear and secrecy it inspires in the families of alcoholics. Occasionally they were started in good faith, by people who honestly believed they had found a "cure" for alcoholism; but as time went on and their "cure" proved to be no cure, some continued just the same, without acknowledging that fact. These are the places which fatten on the fears and hopes of frantic families and desperate alcoholics. People have been known to sell and pawn their belongings to get the necessary money to send an alcoholic to one of these "cures." It is a tragic situation, but it need not continue. When alcoholism is openly discussed, and people can freely seek knowledge and information, such places will quietly disappear. In areas where local branches of the National Council on Alcoholism have opened Alcoholism Information Centers, many questionable places for the treatment of alcoholics have either reorganized to give proper treatment, or have closed down.

It is advisable for the family (or friends—or employer, for it is sometimes he) to consult the best medical opinion they can find to help them choose a suitable place. Even then, they should look into the places suggested, and learn something about their methods of treatment, before sending their alcoholic there—and spending their money. In this way they will at least know what type of care they are buying, and more or less what to expect from it.

Once again let it be said that everything which helps alcoholics recover is of value, and should be widely known. It has already been shown that alcoholics must be willing to accept help before anything can be done for them. Very often it is the family or friends of an alcoholic who bring him to that point of willingness, and must then guide him to specific constructive action. In other cases, having reached readiness himself, the alcoholic turns to family or friends for advice on his next move. Ir either event it is essential that family and friends know of every kind of help which exists, for sometimes many ways have been tried before the right one (for that particular alcoholic) was found; sometimes it was a combination of methods which finally succeeded.

The problem is so vast and complex that no one single method is likely, at this stage of our knowledge, to be one hundred per cent effective with *all* alcoholics. And this may always be true, regardless of what new knowledges we may gain, for *alcoholics are people*—and so they differ. What makes sense to one may seem nonsense to another; what appeals to one may be repugnant to another. Since they are all alcoholics, suffering from the same illness, their goal must be identical: to stop drinking, completely and forever. The means by which they achieve that goal, however, may differ widely, for each of the various methods of treatment mentioned here has had its quota of successful recoveries. The one thing they all have in common is the proof they all offer that alcoholics *can* recover . . . if not by one means, then perhaps by another, or by a combination of several at once.

It would be an ideal treatment center which offered all methods known to have had any success, *and* worked closely with the nearest group of Alcoholics Anonymous. The alcoholic going there for help would be able to work out with the doctors what method they, and he, considered most likely to succeed with him. It might be just one, or first one and then another, or even several at once. But they would all be available in one spot, perhaps even in his own city or town. The establishment of a network of such alcoholic clinics is one of the goals of the National Council on Alcoholism. When that day comes, there will be less need for the lay public to know of all methods of treament in such detail.

11

ALCOHOLICS ANONYMOUS

Alcoholics Anonymous has been called an organization, a society, a movement, a fellowship, a semi-religious group, and a method of treatment. None of these descriptions is wholly accurate, some of them are completely wrong. Alcoholics Anonymous is neither an organization nor a society in the accepted sense of those words. Nor is it a semi-religious group, nor a "movement" —whatever that may be! It is both a fellowship and a method of treatment, but it is also many other things, so that neither word in itself is descriptive enough. To its own members, Alcoholics Anonymous is first a way back to life, and then a design for living. To the outside world it has often been, simply, a miracle.

For the purposes of this book, which is intended for the nonalcoholic world in which the alcoholic lives, a world which must cope with that alcoholic somehow, a description of the functions of Alcoholics Anonymous, and what to expect and not to expect from it, is very much in order. For that world has many erroneous conceptions of A.A., regardless of the fact that almost every-one knows the letters and what they stand for.

This lack of understanding of the functions of A.A. is constantly apparent in the impossible demands which are made upon secretaries of A.A. groups, or individual members of A.A., by desperate families, exasperated employers, baffled professional workers (from ministers and doctors to social and welfare workers), and even by alcoholics themselves. A.A. groups and members have been asked to be detectives and go and find a lost alcoholic; to be doctors and come running in the middle of the night when a frantic wife thought her alcoholic husband was about to die; to be nurses and sit through the end of a bout; to be police and rush to the rescue when an alcoholic turned violent; to be employment agencies and find an alcoholic a job; to be welfare services and take care of an alcoholic's stricken family; and most often of all, to come and talk to an alcoholic who "won't listen to reason," and who has shown no desire whatever to talk to or listen to an A.A. They have also frequently been asked to "take care" of a recalcitrant alcoholic, which actually meant to "police" him and keep him from drinking.

Indignant families have been heard to say, "That Alcoholics Anonymous is a fake. Why, I called them to come and get John sober, and they asked me if *he* wanted to see them. Naturally he didn't or I wouldn't have had to call them. They wouldn't come—what good are they?" Or, "I went over to that A.A. office myself and told them just how terribly Joe was behaving, and they wouldn't do a thing! They said to send him over when *he* was ready! What earthly good is that?" And professional workers have been heard to complain, "I called and told them the whole dreadful situation with the X's, and they said they could do nothing about it unless Mr. X asked for them. What kind of an organization is that?" Or, "That Alcoholics Anonymous won't co-operate. We asked them for a report on Mr. Y, whom we sent to them two months ago, and they said they didn't keep records. Some organization!"

Then there are those who firmly believe that A.A. performs miracles, and expect such miracles to be performed to order. "Just send your husband to A.A., Mrs. B. He'll never touch another drop." Or, "It's easy. They just walk in there and they never drink again—miraculous!" And those who believe that all A.A. members wear halos and wings: "Send for them any time. They'll drop everything and come. They're saints." Or, "He couldn't possibly have lied to you. He can't be drinking. He's an A.A., isn't he?" Those who expect A.A. to possess infallible miraculous powers can be the most bitter when disillusioned. "That A.A. doesn't work. Dick went twice, and he's drunk again." Or, "Who said A.A. was so wonderful? I know three men who went to them and they're still drinking. It's no good, I tell you—just like everything else."

It is not surprising that people expect the impossible from A.A.—it has often done the impossible. It is not surprising that people believe it to possess miraculous powers—it has often seemed to perform miracles. Alcoholics who have been drunk most of the time for thirty years and more have got sober and stayed sober through A.A. Alcoholics who have taken every known treatment, have had thousands of dollars spent on caring for them, have sobered up and begun to take their own responsibilities, and to earn more than was ever spent on their illness, through A.A. People of all ages, from eighteen to eighty; of all backgrounds, from the poorest to the richest and most aristocratic; of all professions and occupations; of both sexes; have recovered from alcoholism and returned to a normal productive life with the help of A.A. How is this done?

In the first place, A.A. has a single purpose from which it will not be diverted, and to which all efforts of A.A. members are directed. In the words of those members, A.A. is a loosely knit, voluntary fellowship of alcoholics (and of alcoholics only) gathered together for the sole purpose of helping themselves and each other to get sober and to stay sober. It is not affiliated or connected in any way with any other group, organization, society, or movement. It is not, for instance, allied to (or fighting) the W.C.T.U. or any other "temperance" group. It has no ties, open, hidden, or otherwise, with the liquor business. In other words it stays completely clear of the age-old Wet-Dry controversy.

Furthermore, A.A. takes no part, as a group, in any organized effort to combat alcoholism on the public-health level, although the public has frequently confused the work of A.A. with the organized effort of the National Council on Alcoholism. In this respect it is important to make clear that A.A. has no official connection with the National Council on Alcoholism, although there is close co-operation between the fellowship of A.A. and this organization. For instance, many A.A. members, *as private individuals,* contribute money to the National Council (usually in small amounts, for most alcoholics are not rich). A.A. members also work on the staff of the National Council, some as regular paid workers, others as volunteers. Others serve on its Board of Directors, which is, however, largely made up of nonalcoholics; and still others help start local committees, of which they become members, although these too are mostly nonalcoholics. These A.A. members, *as individuals,* are trying to use their special interest in and knowledge of alcoholism, for the benefit of the many hundreds of thousands of alcoholics, and their families and friends, who have not yet learned (what the A.A.'s have been fortunate enough to learn) about alcoholism. As a matter of fact, the National Council was founded by a recovered alcoholic, who had the constant advice, guidance, and assistance of the founder of A.A. in the early organization and planning of the Council and its objectives. This is perhaps one of the reasons why so many people confuse A.A. with the National Council on Alcoholism. A full description of the purposes and functions of A.A., and, later, of the National Council and its work, should help to clarify the distinction between the two activities.

A.A., as such, espouses no causes, even causes designed to help alcoholics. It does not sponsor or support hospitals, nursing homes, or sanitariums for alcoholics. It takes no part in any controversial matter. It is not connected or involved with any sect, denomination or creed. It takes no position on any public matter. As a matter of fact it takes no position, as an entity, even on internal matters, although it has evolved a few traditions which have been set down in words, and to which most A.A. members adhere. It has only one condition for membership: an honest desire to stop drinking—a condition which leaves open doors as wide as the world . . . to alcoholics. It is taken for granted that this condition refers to *alcoholic drinking only*. A.A. accepts only alcoholic drinkers as members.

This one condition, however, explains the reasons behind such complaints as are made about A.A. A.A. members do not go out into the highways and byways (or into bars) proselytizing for new members. They wait until the alcoholic himself asks for their help—but if and when he asks, it is given unstintingly, even though he may have a difficult period of indeterminate length during which he "slips around" or "bounces"—in other words, repeatedly relapses into his old drinking pattern. During such a period with an alcoholic who has sincerely asked for help, A.A. members willingly perform all the functions so often asked of them in vain on behalf of an unwilling alcoholic: playing detective, doctor, nurse, policeman and constant companion; giving understanding and sympathetic help at all hours of the day or night; helping out with family problems; sometimes even taking the alcoholic in to live with them. It is these actions which have given rise to false expectations on the part of outsiders who do not fully understand the functions of A.A. But A.A. members, since they are all alcoholics themselves, know very well that if they performed such services for an alcoholic who had never expressed a wish for their help, they might only harm that alcoholic, for they could arouse such resentment against this unwanted "interference" that the alcoholic's readiness to accept help of any kind might be indefinitely postponed. Some A.A. members will willingly advise the family on how best to handle the unwilling alcoholic to help bring him to readiness; other members feel unqualified to do this, and will only work with the alcoholic, not with his family. Families, therefore, who are seeking help from A.A., must find it by attending meetings and learning by listening, or from individual members whom they may meet there, or whom they may know, and who may be willing to advise them. It is not a group function to help anyone other than an alcoholic who seeks that help.

The alcoholic who seeks help, however, will be shown the A.A. way to sobriety. Further, he will be convinced that he too can learn the way, by seeing about him dozens, or hundreds, even thousands in the big cities, who have trod that way successfully before him. This is perhaps the first great lesson the newcomer is taught: that it can be done. He sees with his own eyes numbers of people who have done it, and he hears with his own ears stories that he must believe, of past drinking as bad or worse than his own. One constantly hears newcomers to A.A. murmuring, "If he can do it, I ought to be able to." Of almost equal importance to the newcomer is the obvious fact that these people are apparently *enjoying* their sobriety, something that he had never dreamed could be possible. Once again he thinks: If they can stay sober and enjoy it, perhaps I can, too. Hope becomes a living reality to him, embodied in the persons of the A.A. members he sees and hears and meets.

The next lesson the newcomer is taught is the exact

nature of his problem. No one tells him he is an alcoholic: that is for him to decide, and to tell them. Presumably, if he is asking for help, he has a problem which he has not been able to solve by himself. He may have doubts, however; he may feel that he has come to A.A. merely to find out if he belongs there. That is all right with them— they will help him to find out, if his desire is honest. And most A.A. members rightly feel that if someone has arrived at the point of coming to A.A. to find out if he belongs there, he unquestionably does belong. For they know, from their own experience, that if an individual's own concern about his drinking has gone far enough to lead him to seek help, that drinking has undoubtedly been causing a continuing problem, and is therefore alcoholic drinking. The definition of an alcoholic given in this book is the one most frequently used in A.A. But that is not enough; the newcomer is told that if he is an alcoholic he is suffering from a disease: alcoholism. Alcoholism in turn is defined as: an obsession of the mind, coupled with an "allergy" of the body. It is explained that "allergy" may not be the correct medical term, but that alcoholics apparently have something in their make-up which causes them to react to alcohol differently than other people, something for which the word allergy is at least an understandable term; and that this condition is what makes it impossible for them ever to drink, since there is no cure known for it. All that A.A. can do, the newcomer learns, is to deal with the obsession of the mind which drives the alcoholic to drink even when he knows that he can't and shouldn't and doesn't want to. The A.A. program, he is assured, can teach him to overcome his obsession so that he doesn't need to drink, and indeed so that he eventually will, quite simply, prefer not to drink. Alcoholism is compared to diabetes, which makes the individual unable to handle sugar; and the alcoholic to the diabetic, who must learn to give up sugar, adhere to a rigid diet, and take insulin regularly. The A.A. program, he is told, is his insulin, and he must begin at once to take it, and be prepared to continue taking it for the rest of his life. He is assured that when he learns a little more about it he will find it very pleasant medicine, indeed, and won't in the least mind.

Most newcomers to A.A. have a sponsor. He is sometimes an old friend who took the plunge into A. A. before they were ready to do so. Occasionally he is a former drinking companion whom the alcoholic sought out, after he had been missing from his usual haunts for a while. Often, however, the sponsor is a complete stranger, someone who came to see the suffering alcoholic after he had called a telephone number listed under Alcoholics Anonymous, or after he had written to a Box Number he had heard or read about; or someone he had met when he first walked into an address he had been given or had found in the telephone book. The exact method by which a newcomer is inducted into A.A. depends on this sponsor, but usually it begins by a sharing of drinking experiences, establishing a rapport known only to alcoholics.

If the newcomer has been drinking hard for a considerable time when this first contact is made, the A.A. will try to get medical help for him. In many cities today there are hospital facilities for this purpose; in far too many others there are none, and the neophyte must sweat it out at home. Sometimes the family physician will help, or the A.A. may know a doctor who will treat the suffering alcoholic. Far too often there is no one to help but the A.A. member, who has only his own experience and his sympathy to offer. But out of his experience have come valuable techniques; one of the most valuable of these is known in A.A. as the "twenty-four hour plan." For an alcoholic who is trying to stop drinking on his own, without benefit of medical aids, this plan is invaluable. He is told, simply, not to think beyond the moment, that he has only to go without alcohol today; and that (as he well knows) any alcoholic can go without a drink for one day. Furthermore, each day is to be like that; he is not to swear off drinking for life; he is not to make any promises to anyone, even to himself; he is simply to try not to drink *for today*. There is an extra, hidden value in this technique, as well; at the end of the first day without a drink under this plan, the alcoholic feels a sense of accomplishment he has not known for years. It is often enough to carry him sailing through the second day, and that in turn carries him through the third. Almost before he knows it he has gone without a drink for a week, a month, perhaps for the first time in years. Later he will find that the "twenty-four hour plan" has many more uses than just helping him to stay away from a drink; he will begin to apply it to many of his life problems, with growing effectiveness, and shrinking worry with its resultant nervous tension.

As soon as feasible the sponsor will take his "prospect" to a meeting. There are two kinds of A.A. meetings, and opinion differs as to which kind is best for a new prospect to attend first. The "open" meeting is just that—open to everyone who wants to come: alcoholics of course, but also their families and friends, and any outsiders who may care to attend: doctors, ministers, social workers, or just people who are interested. The idly curious, of whom early A.A. members were very fearful when "open" meetings were first introduced, do not seem to come, or if they do, they change during the course of the meeting from idly curious to impressed and interested. The audience does not participate in an "open" meeting; there is a leader and three or four speakers, each of whom identifies himself (or herself) as an alcoholic, both by stating the fact and by telling some of his drinking experiences. This is done for the specific purpose of letting any "prospects" in the audience know, beyond the shadow of a doubt, that they are listening to people who know firsthand what they are talking about; and to convince those same newcomers that here are no high-flown "preachers" talking down to them and offering them "salvation" from a mountaintop of personal invulnerability. Each speaker hopes that he will personify hope to some alcoholic whose past experiences may have been similar to his own. Usually the speakers recount the steps by which they falteringly reached the haven of A.A., and talk of what that haven has meant to them, how they have used the techniques and principles of A.A., and what their resultant sobriety has done for them and their families. At the end of such a meeting, coffee and refreshments are usually served, and it is then that the newcomer meets and chats with many A.A. members. Some of them will exchange telephone numbers with him, and urge him to call them if he feels he needs support at any moment. Often they will make dates for luncheon or dinner, or to have coffee together at the dangerous cocktail hour. All of them will suggest that he go to as many meetings as possible, at least for a while, although later one a week may be sufficient. He will learn that he is not expected to speak at a meeting for a long while to come, and then only if he is willing; in many A.A. groups no one is allowed to speak at a meeting until he has had three months' sobriety. But most of all he will learn of the warm friendliness that exists among these alcoholics; he will feel not only welcome, but often as if he had come home at last to his own people. He is taken on face value here. No one asks his age, occupation, financial position, background—they rarely even ask his last name, for first names are the rule, at once. No one looks down on him from a height of long sobriety, for there is a saying in A.A. that all members are only one drink away from a drunk, and another that it is the quality and not the quantity of sobriety that counts. The newcomer's few hours of sobriety have as much value in the members' eyes as their own months or years, provided he is serious about making it permanent. It is often said that a newcomer is the most important person at an A.A. meeting: because of his great need; and also because of their need of him, both to learn more of A.A. principles by teaching them to him, and as a link in the endless chain they are forging to pull themselves and other alcoholics out of the abyss of alcoholism.

"Closed" meetings are the second type of meeting held in A.A. These are closed to nonalcoholics, and a newcomer who attends one has thereby taken the first step in A.A.—the admission that he is an alcoholic. The first of the twelve steps that constitute the A.A. program puts it very flatly: "We admitted that we were powerless over alcohol—that our lives had become unmanageable." Closed meetings vary in the precise manner in which they are managed, but they are always discussion meetings, with full audience participation. A newcomer need not speak out, but often does, asking questions about matters under discussion, about things which have troubled him personally, or about A.A. itself. Everyone may say or ask whatever he wishes at a closed meeting, and anyone present may answer. The deepest problems of alcoholics get threshed out here, and experience is shared freely and completely. These meetings, too, are followed by coffee and further discussions in twos and threes. A newcomer can become quickly and widely acquainted in A.A. at meetings.

The twelve steps as such are rarely discussed with a newcomer until he asks to discuss them. He is given a copy of them immediately, either on a card to carry in his wallet, or in a pamphlet which also explains A.A. more fully. But it is recognized that he must digest these slowly, and approach them in his own way. Many A.A. members have been unable to accept the so-called "spiritual steps" of the program even after many months (in a few rare cases even after some years) of successful sobriety. New members are not pushed on this; they are merely asked to "keep an open mind" on the subject, and reminded that whenever the word God is used in those steps it is followed, in italics for emphasis, by the phrase "as we understood Him." The effort is to keep the doors wide open, and allow the alcoholic to find his own way in, as much as possible. Few people take the steps in their written order, for instance, and may not take more than two or three of them for many months. The suggested steps are as follows: 1. We admitted that we were powerless over alcohol—that our lives had become unmanageable. 2. Came to believe that a Power greater than ourselves could restore us to sanity. 3. Made a decision to turn our will and our lives over to the care of God *as we understood Him.* 4. Made a searching and fearless moral inventory of ourselves. 5. Admitted to God, to ourselves and to another human being the exact nature of our wrongs. 6. Were entirely ready to have God remove all these defects of character. 7. Humbly asked Him to remove our shortcomings. 8. Made a list of all persons we had harmed, and became willing to make amends to them all. 9. Made direct amends to such people wherever possible, except when to do so would injure them or others. 10. Continued to take personal inventory and when we were wrong, promptly admitted it. 11. Sought through prayer and meditation to improve our conscious contact with God *as we understood Him,* praying only for knowledge of His will for us and the power to carry that out. 12. Having had a spiritual awakening as the result of these steps, we tried to carry this message to alcoholics and practice these principles in all our affairs.

This looks like a big order to anyone, and particularly to an alcoholic still enmeshed in the problems of years of alcoholic drinking. He is reassured that few members, even those with ten or twelve years of successful membership behind them, feel that they are completely living up to this program. One frequently hears the statement, "I guess it's because I'm honestly *trying* to follow the twelve steps that I've been able to stay sober—I don't suppose I'll ever be able to really live up to them." It is suggested that a new member take those steps which he feels he can take: usually the first one of admission, the eighth and ninth on making amends, and that part of the twelfth dealing with helping other alcoholics, as a starter. Soon he will be discussing the "moral inventory" with his sponsor, or at a closed meeting, and learning that it has nothing to do with "morals" in the usual sense, but rather with an effort to find his own true motives for his actions, to learn his assets and his liabilities as a person, and then to concentrate on using his assets and minimizing his liabilities.

Meanwhile the new member is spending his time with other A.A.'s who are not drinking—his problem of companionship is solved—he need not seek surcease from his intolerable loneliness in bars—he has found people who not only understand, but deeply sympathize with his innermost problems, and are anxious to work out joint solutions, since their own problems are frequently identical or very similar. He begins calling on other alcoholics who have not even taken the first step; he finds that he can help them; that even his tiny bit of sobriety looks tremendous to them; that the little he has learned is new and important to them; he begins to feel some importance as an individual, and his self-respect slowly returns. He is on the way to recovery.

The spiritual basis on which the A.A. program rests

has posed a problem for many alcoholics who were seeking help but feared to approach A.A. because of it. This need not be a barrier to anyone. A.A. members are most definitely *not* psalm-singing, praying proselytizers; it should never be forgotten that they are alcoholics themselves, and that many of them had the same kind of fears and hesitations before they became members. They are, therefore, unlikely to impose on other alcoholics what they once feared would be imposed on them; and they understand better than most what those fears are. A.A. members come from all kinds of religious backgrounds: Protestant, Catholic, Jewish, and none at all. There have been one or two professed Buddhists who became members; some Chinese who were brought up in the ways of Confucius; Hindus; and Parsees who are Zoroastrians; and as A.A. spreads over the world, which it is rapidly doing, there will one day be no creed, sect, denomination, faith or philosophy which is not represented. This alone would prevent any proselytizing in a religious sense, if nothing else did.

Remarkably enough, there are never *religious* arguments or even discussions among A.A. members. Each person is assumed to have his own approach to religion, and it is considered strictly his own business. On broad spiritual matters, including ethics and philosophy, there are many discussions, but questions are invariably met with very tentative suggestions, never with "musts." One reason for this delicate handling of a possibly explosive subject, is the recognition in A.A. of the danger of anger and resentment to an alcoholic. There is an A.A. saying that an alcoholic plus a resentment equals a drunk, as

surely as two and two equals four. And there is another
A.A. saying which has bearing on this subject: "Live and
let live." The same delicate and tentative approach is
used on sexual or marital problems, which are considered
strictly the affair of the individual.

In short, the whole A.A. approach is a highly individual one. Interference in the life of a new member is
not countenanced, and most A.A. members shy away
from even strongly invited participation in the newcomer's problems, other than with alcohol. On that level,
however, they will go the whole hog, and they will also
do all they can to help out with job-hunting. If a member
gets into trouble, the family can usually count on his
A.A. friends to do all in their power to help the situation,
in every possible way. But it is individual help given by
individual A.A. members, not by the A.A. group as such.

A.A. groups are not organized in any usual sense. As
soon as the membership grows beyond twenty-five or
thirty, there is likely to be a Steering Committee (rotating, so that all members serve at some time) to conduct
necessary business, such as hiring a meeting place, and
planning open meetings. There are no fees or dues in
A.A.—it costs exactly nothing to become a member (save
the unbelievably high initiation fee paid during years of
alcoholic drinking). But when a group has grown beyond
the confines of the members' living rooms, the hat is
passed at meetings to raise the rent for the hall. Then a
Treasurer is elected to handle this sum, and a Secretary
(both of these are also rotating offices) to take care of
written inquiries, and to correspond, on behalf of the
group, with the A.A. Central Service Office in New

York. This Central Service Office is the international headquarters of A.A., where inquiries are received from all over the world.[1] It is supported by a part of the hat-passing collections, but its main support comes from the proceeds of the sale of the book, *Alcoholics Anonymous*, which every new member wants to own (he can buy it on a ten-cents-a-week plan if he wishes—or borrow one until he can buy his own). This book is owned and published by Alcoholics Anonymous. A.A. accepts no outside contributions for its work, and takes great pride in being self-supporting. Many large groups in big cities have found it necessary to establish their own local Central Office to handle inquiries for the area. When this happens, a Secretary (or two or three) is usually hired at a reasonable salary to run the office, and since most of the work is with alcoholics, potential members, the Secretary is usually an A.A. member, who is obviously better qualified to do this work than a nonalcoholic. The General Secretaries in the Central Service Office are also A.A. members, for the same reason. These are the only paid jobs in A.A., for the major work is done voluntarily by the members, as much for their own sake as for the person they are helping.

None of these offices keep records in the sense that a social or welfare office would keep records. There are no case histories, no careful statistics on recoveries, failures, or in-and-outers. Smaller groups sometimes keep an informal roster of membership, so that the Secretary can send a written inquiry to a member who lives nearby, or

---

[1] Inquiries should be addressed to: Alcoholics Anonymous, P.O. Box 459, Grand Central Annex, New York 17, N. Y.

know where to reach the right member for a particular call, or the nearest member for an emergency call. But when a group has grown large enough to have its own Central Office, that office does not keep a file of names and addresses, with length of sobriety filled in. It directs inquiries to the volunteer elected secretaries of neighborhood groups, who, in turn, turn the call over to a member known personally to them, unless they take it themselves. The semiannual count of A.A. membership is made by these local secretaries of small groups, who simply forward to the Central Service Office the number of active members of their own group. On this count, the early 1957 figures showed approximately two hundred thousand members of A.A., and close to seven thousand groups in the United States, Canada, and seventy foreign countries.

To sum up, then, the program of Alcoholics Anonymous, which has proved so successful with so many alcoholics hitherto regarded as hopeless, can be divided into two parts, totalling ten points. The first five consist of what A.A. does for the alcoholic; and the second five, what A.A. teaches the alcoholic to do for himself:

1. Hope plus proof is given. This is made concrete in the person of the sober member who calls on the prospect, or by the sight of a roomful of cheerful, usually prosperous-looking, and obviously sober people, at a meeting.
2. Information on what alcoholism is, and what constitutes an alcoholic, is supplied, sometimes for the first time. The recognition of what is wrong with him, that he

is a sick person, suffering from a definite disease, often lifts an unbearable burden of guilt and shame from the alcoholic's mind, which makes it possible for him to think about recovery and to take action toward it. The importance of this can hardly be overestimated.

3. Identification is established, first with one person, the sponsor, then with a group of people, at a meeting. This shows the alcoholic, again (often for the first time), that he is not alone and "different" from all the world. To know that there are others, many others, like himself, is of vast importance to the usually isolated alcoholic. It is also of vital importance to him to feel a part *of* something, for he has long felt apart *from* everything, cut off from the world, and from humankind.

4. A social milieu is provided for him. He is immediately accepted on an equal level with the other members, and drawn into all activities pertaining to A.A. There can be no left-out feeling (from which he has sometimes suffered all his life). No shame is necessary; his behavior while drinking is considered a part of his illness, and not an indication of his true character. His lonely hours are filled, partly by meetings, partly by "twelfth-step work" with other alcoholics, partly by ordinary social intercourse with other A.A. members, all of whom spend a great deal of time in each other's company, doing all the things that everyone does in his social life. Through this acceptance of himself as an ordinary human being, the alcoholic's self-respect and self-confidence begin to return to him.

5. The twelve steps give him a concrete program of action, "something he can get his teeth into" and begin

working on at once. Most important is the fact that he does not have to do all this entirely alone: "Let's do it together" is a byword in A.A.

6. The things A.A. teaches the alcoholic to do for himself begin with the "twenty-four hour plan." Here he immediately finds a daily sense of accomplishment, something he usually has not felt for years. There is also great relaxation for him in the limited effort he has to make—he has usually been straining at the, to him, impossible goal of trying to control his drinking, or swearing off "forever."

7. Group therapy is actually practiced in A.A. closed meetings, even though without a psychiatrically trained leader. The A.A. members who lead these discussion meetings have had their training through their own alcoholic and A.A. experience.

8. "Twelfth-step work" is one of the most vital steps in the process of recovery through A.A. It provides what many doctors order for their alcoholic patients: a hobby, or a new compelling interest; for nothing is more fascinating to alcoholics than other alcoholics, especially when they feel they can help them. This feeling of being able to help, of at last being useful to humanity, is one of the greatest products of "twelfth-step work." The alcoholic is now engaged in vital rehabilitation work, work that no one else can do quite as well as he: a healthy feeling of his dignity and importance as a human being is growing in him. His guilt feelings—which were partially lifted by the discovery that he was not peculiar or bad, but that his irrational behavior was the usual result of an illness over which he, without help, had no control—are

further dissipated as that very behavior of his drinking past provides his most useful tools with which to help others. Each time he wins a new prospect's confidence with a story of his own past antics, the horror he had felt at the memory of that antic recedes. He can live with himself now, past and all. His interest in the new prospects he is trying to help turns outward, and away from his past obsessive self-concern; he is becoming extroverted, and with this usually comes a gradual lessening of the egocentricity which so strongly marks the alcoholic.

9. Working together with a group brings him fully back into the human family. As he takes a more and more active part in A.A., he is integrating himself into a social pattern, sometimes for the first time in his life, more often for the first time in years. He has to learn to "give and take" with other equally "difficult" personalities, very like his own, who are learning the same things at the same time. This often causes friction and explosions within A.A. groups; but it is a good and necessary part of the process of recovery, and valuable lessons are always learned from such episodes. Group problems deriving from this are known in A.A. as "growing pains"; problems within a group are also growing pains, of the individuals concerned. Learning to accept all these things as part of the recovery process helps the alcoholic learn to adjust to reality. What he learns in his new life as an A.A. he soon begins to apply outside of A.A., and he finds that it works there, too. Soon he will begin to feel able to handle life, whatever its problems, just as well as he is learning to handle his urge to drink.

10. The spiritual basis of A.A. actually permeates all of

the foregoing steps, even for the alcoholic who doesn't think he has accepted it. For the changes in attitude which are implicit in all the above are of a spiritual nature, as well as being mental and emotional. The alcoholic who has found faith in his sponsor, and then in his group, has already become dependent on a power greater than himself, even if it does not yet have a capital P. As time goes on his faith will extend to a new faith in humanity, and from this it is not usually very far to a faith in the Creator of that humanity. Many A.A.'s have learned at first hand of the miraculous powers of prayer; many have found great inner peace and happiness in a full return to their church; many others have embraced a formal faith for the first time; some have found their own private faith which sustains them well. All save a very few give full credit to spiritual help in overcoming their alcoholic obsession.

With a program of such vast possibilities for helping countless alcoholics through its chain-reaction nature, it could be asked why we should bother with any other treatment. There are two main reasons: First, not every alcoholic is willing to try A.A., although he might be willing to undergo some other form of treatment. Since the objective should be to help alcoholics recover, by whatever method will best work *for them*, it behooves us to know all there is to know about every method which has had any success, and to use whatever method seems best suited to the particular case. Second, A.A. has never claimed anything like 100 per cent recoveries, although it does believe that considerably more than 50 per cent of those who have tried it have recovered. Since it does not keep records, recovery figures can not be verified, and one hears everything from 50 per cent to 85 per cent from A.A. members. This latter figure may even be a fair figure in some groups, which have been going long enough to have finally helped some who came and went away long ago, and who returned at last, to stay. But even if accurate figures existed, and even if they showed only a 50 per cent recovery rate, this would be an incredibly high record, considering that alcoholism was regarded until very recently as a hopeless affliction.

It must also be remembered that A.A. keeps its doors very wide, and takes on all comers at their own say-so. There is no filtering out of people who do not rightly belong in the classification of alcoholics; of people who are mentally ill, or are psychopathic personalities, or have been permanently damaged beyond repair. Such cases may well account for many so-called "failures," or seemingly permanent "slippees" (people who relapse constantly, although they return after each relapse). And because of the lack of records no one knows how many— who first came because they were forced, by a wife or a boss, or the fear of losing wife or job, and went away to drink some more—have come back again to stay, or will come back someday. Then there are so-called failures, or "slippees," who have a real neurosis, which either preceded or was the result of their alcoholism, and for whom A.A. alone is not enough. With some psychiatric help many of these people could probably go on to successful membership in A.A., for it offers them many things which psychiatry cannot supply.

When the day comes that alcoholism is accepted for what it is—one of our greatest scourges, but a disease which can be treated—and when we treat it with all our resources, as we do other illnesses, then A.A. will be able to function to its full potentialities. With the understanding and co-operation of the general public; with the availability of Alcoholism Information and Consultation Centers to bridge the abyss of shame and fear, and to give practical assistance; with hospitals open to acute cases, and adequate clinical facilities for diagnosis and treatment; there might be very few failures among those who went to A.A. for help. And with a growing alcoholic population, estimated at five million or more in 1958, that is a day which is long overdue.

12

A RESOURCE FOR
EVERYONE—NCA

The day of deliverance outlined above is not so far away as it may seem. Public awareness is growing by leaps and bounds, and real understanding will not be far behind. More and more people want to "*do* something"; more and more groups and organizations are seeking information, and advice on instituting action. And finally, more and more individuals are seeking information and guidance about a particular alcoholic—sometimes themselves. How did this come about, and where can they all go for the help they want?

There is at least a partial answer to both questions in the National Council on Alcoholism, Inc. (NCA), with headquarters in the New York Academy of Medicine Building.[1] A further answer lies in NCA's network of local affiliates.[2]

---

[1] The National Council on Alcoholism—2 East 103rd St., New York 29, N. Y.

[2] Directory of local affiliates may be obtained by writing NCA.

NCA was founded in 1944 in an atmosphere of almost total darkness. The word "alcoholism" was a taboo word. The public attitude was compounded of ignorance, fear, prejudice and hostility, and the public attitude included most professional attitudes. The "drunkard" was considered a hopeless proposition, and wholly to blame for his own condition. Almost nothing was being done about alcoholism, except by alcoholics themselves (A.A.) and a few courageous scientists at Yale. Obviously they were working against tremendous obstacles.

The new organization (then called the National Committee for Education on Alcoholism) was dedicated to removing those obstacles, and to creating an atmosphere of understanding and co-operation in which constructive work on alcoholism, and for alcoholics, could go forward. NCA's slogan was, and is, *"to arouse public opinion and mobilize it for action."* But only in the field of alcoholism—*not* in the wider area of alcohol. NCA is neither "wet" nor "dry," and is not concerned with social drinking. It is a voluntary health agency devoted to the disease of alcoholism, and it defines its purposes as follows:

GENERAL

To deal with alcoholism in the same general fashion as other public health agencies combat tuberculosis, cancer, heart disease and other major threats to human health.

SPECIFIC

1. To conduct an education and public information program on alcoholism as a disease and public health problem
2. To initiate constructive action at the community level through the organization and affiliation of local committees on alcoholism
3. To provide advisory and other services for agencies concerned with alcoholism, particularly local committees
4. To stimulate appropriate action in this field by appropriate groups and organizations, so that the responsibility for combating alcoholism may be shared by all
5. To provide consultation, advisory and other services to such groups and organizations
6. To initiate, to support, and to conduct research into all means that might lead to the prevention and control of alcoholism
7. To provide literature and other written materials for the use of all interested individuals, groups, and organizations

This calls for a vast variety of activities, carried on by NCA's staff, at the home office and throughout the country. NCA reaches out still further through the distribution of literature (shipped at the rate of half a million pieces a year). Much of this material goes in bulk to the local affiliates where it is widely distributed by their Alcoholism Information Centers.

Not least among NCA's activities is the provision of a central source of sound, unbiased and up-to-date information on all aspects of alcoholism and activities concerning it: a source readily available to any individual, organization, or group, by mail, by telephone, or in per-

son. Inquiries dealing with specialized or technical matters are promptly referred to the proper source. Services
sought by residents of an area where there are local resources, which may be a local affiliate of NCA, or a
state or municipal program, are referred to the local
source. It is NCA's business to stimulate the creation of
more and more such local resources, in order to make
immediate help more easily available to those in need,
wherever they may live.

In short, the National Council on Alcoholism, which
is the only national voluntary agency in this field, serves
the public in the same broad areas of education, research
and services, as do other health agencies such as the
National Tuberculosis Association, the American Heart
Association, the National Association on Mental Health,
and the American Cancer Society, each in its own special
field.

NCA has many similarities, in organization, purposes
and functions, to the well-known organizations just
named. It also has some striking differences. Only in the
field of alcoholism is there a huge and active organization
of former sufferers from a particular disease, banded
together to help other sufferers recover, and famous
throughout the land (A.A). Only in this field are there
two large national bodies, each with local groups across
the country, each solely concerned with alcoholism and
alcoholics, each complementing the other's activities, and
co-operating with each other wherever possible. It is
small wonder that a public new to the very word "alcoholism," should mix them up. Add to this the growing
number of state Commissions on Alcoholism, or Divi-

sions on Alcoholism, or other names by which state alcoholism programs are known, and it is easy to see why many people lump them all together, and call them all by the easiest of the names to remember: A.A.

Because of this it should prove helpful to answer some of the questions that are so frequently asked of us who work in this field: questions as to the difference between NCA and A.A.; questions as to why NCA does not receive government support; questions as to the separate functions of NCA (a *voluntary* agency), and official state alcoholism programs.

It could be said that NCA grew out of the needs of A.A., whose single purpose has already been stated, and that NCA was designed to do those things for alcoholism which A.A. could not, and did not wish to do. Education of the public, for instance; the treatment of acute alcoholism in general hospitals; adequate clinical facilities; and services to nonalcoholics, especially families, friends, employers, etc. There is a great difference in means of support, too. The National Council on Alcoholism requires money—large sums of money—to carry on its broad program, and like other voluntary agencies it must go to the public for that support, must conduct fund-raising drives. Alcoholics Anonymous, on the other hand, is entirely supported by its own members, and will not accept donations from other sources. A.A. has frequently returned such unsought contributions to the donors, even when they were bequests from a donor now deceased, sometimes with the suggestion that the gift be made to the National Council on Alcoholism, if possible.

There is a close working relationship between the loosely knit fellowship of A.A. and the formal organization of NCA, a relationship that is good for the cause of alcoholism in a myriad of ways.

The question of government support has to do with the basic differences between voluntary and official agencies. The two are entirely different in many ways, beginning with their means of support. The word "voluntary" means just that money is raised by seeking voluntary contributions, from individuals, corporations and foundations. In addition, the people who serve on the voluntary agency's policy-making Board of Directors, or Trustees, are volunteers, giving their services without compensation, and free to make decisions independent of any consideration other than the best interests of the organization they serve.

Official agencies, on the other hand, whether Federal, state, or local, are supported by tax monies appropriated to their use for legally specified purposes. The appropriation is sometimes written into the law, but more often is voted afterwards by official legislative bodies: Congress, state legislatures, or local legislators, who are elected, receive compensation for their public service, and must carry out the law which created and defined the activities of the official agency concerned.

Voluntary organizations by their very nature, therefore, are not eligible for appropriations of tax monies, nor do they receive direct support from official government agencies. In certain narrowly specified areas, however, an official agency may make a special grant to a voluntary agency for a specific purpose. The United States Public Health Service, for instance, will underwrite certain professional conferences or institutes, or make a grant to a particular research project, if these undertakings fit into their own legally defined purposes and objectives, and gain their approval. But no funds derived from taxes are or can be appropriated or granted to voluntary agencies for their general operating expenses, since their programs and policies are determined by a volunteer group of citizens serving on independent Boards which are not under government or official direction or control.

These points serve to underline the basic difference —and the separate functions—of NCA and its affiliates (voluntary agencies), and the state and municipal alcoholism programs.

The role of the voluntary agency can be very flexible and very broad, limited only by its ability to raise the necessary funds. Since it is under no legislative restrictions, it is not bound by prevailing public opinion as manifested by the public's elected representatives. This freedom has allowed the voluntary health agencies to act as leaders, to create new public attitudes (as in t.b., cancer, mental health), which in turn have caused the public to demand and to get progressive action by their elected representatives.

The voluntary agency is also free to experiment in new ways of meeting their particular problem, to take the calculated risk that some of these experiments may prove to be failures. Where such experiments succeed, however (and they very often do), they are likely to be taken over by the official agencies, since they can more easily get tax monies appropriated to carry on projects or to institute methods already proved successful.

This is the American pattern, set by the National Tuberculosis Association early in this century, and followed by both voluntary and official health agencies ever since. The National Council on Alcoholism is following this well-marked American way.

13

WHAT TO DO ABOUT AN ALCOHOLIC

There are a number of general rules about how to deal with an alcoholic, which apply to anyone, whether the individual is closely related (wife, husband, mother, father, sister, brother, son or daughter), or just a near relation (in-laws, cousins, etc.); or a friend or neighbor; or a business colleague, employer, or employee; or merely an acquaintance, or someone working in the same office, shop, or factory. For all of these people, who make up the world in which the alcoholic lives, the *first rule* is: *inform yourself*.

Sources of information have been clearly spelled out in preceding chapters. There is a major source of understanding, however, which has not been pointed up: attendance at open meetings of Alcoholics Anonymous. People concerned with alcoholics, or with a particular alcoholic, can learn more about the nature of the problem with which they are dealing in this way than in any other. Here alcoholics speak freely about themselves, their actions, their thoughts, and their true feelings, and they speak publicly, for the benefit of all who will listen. Outsiders with an honest interest or concern are welcomed, and many professional people regularly avail themselves of this opportunity to learn about alcoholics from the best possible source—alcoholics themselves.

Such meetings are regularly held in most cities and towns of America today, and A.A. is usually listed in the telephone book, sometimes with an answering service which will give the time and place of the next meeting. There are a few A.A. groups, usually in small communities, which do not hold open meetings, however, and in such cases it would be necessary to know a member personally, and to request an invitation to attend. If this is not feasible, then the National Council on Alcoholism remains the best source of information. In any case, it is the major source of literature especially prepared for the nonalcoholic layman.

Wherever possible, it is strongly recommended to anyone who knows an alcoholic he would like to help, that he attend at least a few A.A. meetings. No matter how much he has read, or what other sources of information he has tapped, he will learn more about alcoholics— and alcoholism—at an A.A. meeting than anywhere else. Here he will come to understand the why of many of the suggestions given in this book. Here, also, he will be reassured that there is hope for his own alcoholic, and he will probably hear stories very like his own.

A new resource is becoming more widely available also: Alanon Family Group meetings. The Alanon Family

Groups have come into being to meet a very real need: direct help to members of the family (wives, husbands, sisters, mothers, grown children) of an alcoholic who has joined A.A. and is himself attending A.A. closed meetings. Families of alcoholics who have not yet accepted A.A. are also welcome at these meetings, and can benefit greatly not only from the things they learn there, but also from the support they gain in handling their problem. Attendance at these meetings is strongly recommended to anyone else who is trying to help an alcoholic.

The *second rule* of importance is: *develop an attitude in keeping with the facts you have learned.* Lip service to the idea of alcoholism as a disease is not enough. The world in which the alcoholic lives must *act* as if it believed this, and must display at all times an attitude which bears out this belief. This is not self-abnegation and martyrdom for those who suffer from the alcoholic's behavior: it is rather pressure constantly brought to bear upon the alcoholic to do something about his condition. Most of us in the United States were brought up with definite ideas of hygiene, and of what to do if we thought we were ill. We have been conditioned to taking care of our health, and to using the medical services available to us when we thought we needed them. We were taught as children in school that we had a responsibility to ourselves and others in regard to our health, and most of us live up to that responsibility in case of illness. Up to now the alcoholic has been made to feel shame if he could not handle his drinking *by himself.* Our goal must be to reverse that: to make him feel shame at not seeking help for his illness. If he himself really comes to believe that he has a disease, the chances are greatly enhanced that he will seek treatment for it. Thousands of cases have proved this.

All nonalcoholics have a great responsibility to remove the stigma and the taboo which have hitherto been attached to alcoholism. This has helped drive the alcoholic, and his family, to secrecy and away from possible assistance. The alcoholic should never be made to feel shame because he is an alcoholic, any more than a diabetic should be made ashamed because of being a diabetic. The nonalcoholic world in which the alcoholic lives must include in its new attitude an acceptance and an openness about the subject of alcoholism; must be as ready to discuss it *objectively* as they are ready to discuss appendicitis, or pneumonia. One of the questions most frequently asked of authorities on alcoholism is "How can I talk to him about it? I can't (or daren't) bring the subject up." Why not? It is an extremely interesting subject. People often talk at length about cancer, or heart disease, or appendicitis; it would be of enormous value if they would talk about alcoholism. Not, of course, pointing out that the person they are talking to is, in their opinion, an alcoholic; but rather a very general discussion which, if properly handled, could well bring admissions from the alcoholic. At the very least it could cause him to do some thinking, particularly if information has been mentioned which is new to him, and an attitude displayed which bears no tincture of disgust, contempt or impatience, and shows nothing that will make him feel shame, disgrace, or degradation. In such discussions, however, it should be made perfectly clear by the nonalcoholic participants that they feel strongly regarding anyone with an illness who refuses to do anything about it; such as a diabetic who allows himself to waste away, refusing to have a diagnosis and learn what is causing his condition, or, having had the diagnosis and learned the bitter truth, refuses to follow the rigid regime necessary to keep him alive and allow him to lead a normal life. They could argue that it is no less than an affront to humanity, in these enlightened days of modern medicine, and in the light of modern knowledge, for a sick person to allow himself to deteriorate and die before everyone's eyes, when something could be done for him if he were willing. Such discussion should always remain general, and never point the finger at any participant or silent hearer; examples used should as much as possible be drawn from other diseases as well as alcoholism, particularly diabetes because of its many similarities to alcoholism, but also tuberculosis, cancer, etc., etc. It is not surprising how many times such general discussions have led alcoholics directly to seek help, and even more often have planted the seed which weeks or months later grew into constructive action on the part of a hitherto recalcitrant alcoholic.

People who have followed the first two rules given here, who have informed themselves and adopted an attitude bearing out that information, can scarcely continue perpetuating the old myths regarding drinking. Some of these are extremely dangerous to alcoholics, and the knowledge that their particular world believes them can effectively prevent their taking any action. Perhaps the most virulent is the myth that an ability to drink great quantities is a sign of virility. This myth, of course, dates from ancient times when wine was associated with blood, and a great drinker of wine was believed to have greatly strengthened himself thereby. To hold such a belief in modern times is little short of ridiculous, yet intelligent grown men, who otherwise are complete products of our comparatively enlightened times, fall for this ancient fairy tale over and over again. They indicate their foolishness by taunting people who can not drink as much as they, calling them "pantywaists," "sissies," "weaklings," and a host of similar opprobrious terms. Such simpleness can be excused in adolescent boys, who don't know any better (although there is little excuse for not teaching them the facts); but it is laughable (and sometimes tragic) coming from grown men and women.

Another myth which is equally dangerous to alcoholics is that of associating drinks with hospitality, so that a "good" host feels that he must press drinks on his guests, often with impolite insistence. How often does one hear remarks such as, "You must taste this—it's a specialty of the house," or, "I'll be offended if you don't have just one—it's the very best (Scotch or rye or Daiquiri or vintage wine or whatever)," or, "Just have one—it can't possibly hurt you, it's my best mixture." This, too, derives from ancient times when wine was associated with ritual, and hospitality was a ritual; also when wine was precious and not everyone was able to offer it, so that the offer showed the host's importance and affluence. This myth received a whole new impetus in America, from Prohibition, for once again, liquor was precious and difficult to obtain, and hosts were proud of what they could get and offer. But it has literally no reason for existence today, when anyone can buy any kind of alcoholic beverage, and when hospitality can be better shown in a thousand other ways. Incidentally, true hospitality never includes putting pressure on one's guests to do or take anything they have once refused. In the case of an alcoholic who may be trying not to drink, such insistence can be a cruel and unfriendly act, for it may break his hard-won resistance and throw him into a relapse. It is hard to believe that anyone would want to be responsible for causing a tubercular to have a hemorrhage; but that is exactly the equivalent of what people daily do to alcoholics, usually, of course, without being aware of it in the slightest.

The nonalcoholic world can make equally bad mistakes in the opposite direction, with the very best intentions. And this brings us to the *third rule*: *never harp on the alcoholic's condition*. It is better not to bring it up at all unless he does. Alcoholics are extremely sensitive about their inability to handle drinking "like other people"; their life is a constant struggle to keep that "difference" hidden. It humiliates and angers them to have it pointed out, and this in turn raises their wall of defiance against the nonunderstanding (nonalcoholic) world still higher, and makes any attempt to reach and help them more difficult. Many alcoholics have been prevented from taking action about themselves by a succession of episodes with family and friends; where drinks were not served to anyone because of their presence; or liquor was no longer kept in the house; or drinks were served, with a (to them) screamingly obvious glass of tomato juice, ginger ale or

Coca Cola on the tray, which was then passed to them last, with nothing else left on it. The alcoholic should be treated like anyone else, insofar as possible, with any gestures of refusal left up to him to make. And if he makes them, no particular attention should be paid to it, either then or later, by anyone, including a delighted wife or husband.

This nonchalant behavior on the part of the nonalcoholic world surrounding the alcoholic should also be shown if he stops drinking, either "going on the wagon" by himself, or by undergoing treatment. His new behavior should be taken as a matter of course, and he should be treated as an intelligent human being who simply chooses, for reasons of his own, not to drink. If he happens to have joined Alcoholics Anonymous, he will undoubtedly want to talk about it, if not immediately, then very soon; but with other methods of recovery, this is not so often the case. And the early period of an alcoholic's sobriety is usually very difficult for him; he is afraid of people, and of how they will make him feel; he can not bear to be made conspicuous, or to feel foolish. Also, until he himself feels sure of his own sobriety, he usually does not wish to have it discussed or pointed out. The attitude of the world in which he lives is vitally important during this period: it could be said that its occupants hold a good measure of his failure or success in their hands and on their tongues. There are plenty of recovered alcoholics who have recovered *in spite of* their families and friends, and they actually deserve double credit. But they should not have to overcome this extra

hazard: recovery is difficult enough, even with all outside forces combining to help in the most thoughtful and
intelligent manner.

A *fourth general rule* is actually implicit in all the
foregoing: *never lecture, or preach*. It is important to remember a number of things about the alcoholic's own
attitude toward his drinking and his resultant behavior.
Almost without exception alcoholics are guilt-ridden to
an extent undreamed-of by outsiders. They begin to feel
guilty from the moment they realize that their drinking
is different from other people's, and that they cannot
always control it at will. As their behavior deteriorates
and shows expanding symptoms, their guilt increases. No
one knows better than they what they are doing to themselves, and to everyone whom they love, and who loves
them. This knowledge is a torture and a torment inde-
scribable to nonalcoholics. Lecturing and preaching,
therefore, are exactly equivalent to rubbing coarse salt
into a gaping wound. They are truly unbearable, and violent reactions simply must result. The alcoholic will do
and promise anything at all to stop such suffering, but
usually the quickest way he knows to stop it is to seek
oblivion in drunkenness. Therefore lecturing (or preaching) is the best possible way to send an alcoholic on a
protracted drunk, which is certainly not the goal of the
lecturer or preacher. There is a further reason (if any
other is needed) for avoiding this. Most alcoholics feel
that the world does not understand them—and they have
been right. Since the nonalcoholic world does not understand them, it cannot, in their opinion, very well help
them. Lecturing and preaching merely confirm this be-

lief of theirs, and harden it into a violent resistance to anything that is suggested to them from such quarters. This in turn obviously makes it impossible for anyone who has lectured them or preached at them, to help them, even if sound methods to suggest are discovered at a later date. The nonalcoholic world can, however, overcome much of the resistance that has been built up by past mistakes if it will adopt a new attitude and actually live up to it, regardless of anything and everything the alcoholic may do, over a considerable period of time. Many families of alcoholics have been in this position and have rightly felt that they seemed the last people in the world their alcoholic would listen to. This was true, but they have frequently been able to change the atmosphere, with resultant ability to gradually bring their alcoholic to seek help.

Another part of this fourth rule against lecturing and preaching is: never take the attitude which usually accompanies such actions, commonly known as the "holier-than-thou" attitude. It is, of course, quite possible to take this attitude while maintaining a tight-lipped silence, and therefore to feel that since one has neither lectured nor preached, one has followed the rule. It is important here to remember that alcoholics are generally highly sensitive people, and can sense an attitude even when it is hidden behind words which say something quite different, or is supposedly concealed behind silence. In this particular sense, alcoholics are very like children, who judge people's feelings and reactions toward them by fleeting expressions and tones of voice, rather than by the words addressed to them. It is very hard to fool an alcoholic on how you really feel about him, and this is one of the main reasons why lip service to the ideas expounded here is not enough. The attitude of sympathetic understanding must be real; if it bears any traces of scorn, contempt, or skepticism, the alcoholic will know it, and react accordingly.

The *final general rule* is: *don't threaten.* At least, don't threaten unless you intend to carry out the threat. There are undoubtedly many cases where drastic action is necessary: such as the wife leaving for the sake of the children, or for her own sake; or the boss firing an alcoholic, after repeated warnings; or friends refusing to see an alcoholic any more. But when such threats are made, as warnings, they must be carried out the very next time the warning is disregarded, else the alcoholic will pay no attention to any further threats, and will make himself believe that nothing will ever happen. Then, when at last it does, he will be filled with unreasoning resentment and self-pity, which will drive him deeper into his alcoholism; for he has been allowed to build a dream castle of his own immunity, and he cannot bear to see it demolished.

In addition to these general rules, there are many specific suggestions which can be given to people in particular situations; and these in turn can be generalized for a number of such situations.

If You Are the Wife of an Alcoholic

All the general rules given here apply to you. It is in fact a matter of life and death that you inform yourself, as fully and as specifically as possible. At all costs you must avoid the "Home Treatment," with its tragic and useless mistakes born out of a complete ignorance about alcoholism. You know now that there are sources of even more detailed information than can be given here, information specifically to fit your particular situation. Avail yourself of it, as soon as possible.

When you have absorbed all the information you can get—sound, unbiased information, not myths or fancies or old wives' tales delivered *ad nauseam* by (perhaps) well-meaning Job's Comforters—then set out to adopt a new attitude. This should produce new behavior on your part, which in turn may easily produce new behavior on the part of your alcoholic. Don't expect this to happen overnight. It may take long and difficult effort on your part, but if it works, it's worth it.

While sedulously avoiding the "Home Treatment," remember never to confiscate the family liquor supply. Above all, don't throw it down the sink—it's simply a waste of good money, for the alcoholic will merely procure more, probably twice as much, spending twice as much money. Furthermore, he will undoubtedly get out of the house to do this, and may not come home for days. This particular action will inevitably hurt you much more than it does him, in the end, and it certainly won't help him at all.

Talk to someone about the situation: a doctor, or minister; perhaps a social worker, or a friend you can trust. You need to spill some of your worries and accumulated resentments if you are to be able to treat your alcoholic like a sick person. Left unexpressed, many of the

feelings you have been harboring will fester, and you
will eventually be as sick a person as your alcoholic. This
happens all too frequently. It is essential for your own
sake, as well as his, that you learn to face the situation
openly. If you begin to face it, he will be more likely to,
but equally important is the fact that facing it is the only
way for you to prepare for constructive action about it.
Above all you must not hide, nor must you "cover up"
for him, even when you feel that it is necessary to help
him hold his job, and that job is your—and your children's—bread and butter. If you have started a constructive program of thought and action, you should be able
to recognize that, perhaps, losing his job is the jolt he
needs to make him take action. Furthermore, hiding is
going to hurt you, turn you in on yourself and away from
the world, and this is already his condition; two in one
family is too much, and since you are the nonalcoholic,
and presumably not sick, it is up to you at this point to
lead him out of his morass; you cannot do this by getting
in with him.

Don't, above all, feel ashamed or degraded. There is
no reason for you to feel these unpleasant emotions, any
more than you would feel them if your husband were
stricken with cancer, or discovered that he had multiple
sclerosis, or if you realized that he was mentally cracking
up. Besides, if you feel these things, you will communi-
cate your feelings to him, with resulting inability to help
him. Also, you will be unable to talk about it, for a sense
of shame and degradation seals the lips, and it is important that you learn to talk about it as objectively as possible, just as you might talk about a simple operation

that your husband needed, and was putting off. Of course, you might well nag him about such an operation, but it would be most unwise to nag him about his alcoholism, since it is more than likely that he would then immediately retaliate by getting drunker than usual. He might also react that way the first few times you talked, even very generally and objectively, about drinking and alcoholism; but if he finds that you are not pointing the finger at him each time you mention it, he may even join in and ask questions.

Go to some A.A. meetings (you needn't tell him you are going, or even where you have been) and learn how alcoholics themselves feel about their problem. You will also learn how other wives of alcoholics feel, and hear stories of how they dealt with it. There, too, you will be able to meet the wives of alcoholics who have recovered, or who are trying not too successfully, or who, like your own, have not yet begun. If you can make friends with some of these women, you will no longer feel so alone, lost and bewildered. They have been through exactly the same things, and they can help you.

Go to Alanon. This organization is especially for you. The wives—and husbands—of alcoholics, whom you will meet there, know your troubles better than you know them yourself. And they know *you*—how you feel, and how you have probably reacted to your situation. They cannot help your husband, and they won't pretend to, but they can help you; which, in turn, may very well help your husband to accept help. Meanwhile you will gain support and strength, if only through realizing that "you are not alone." If there is not an Alanon Family

Group in your city or town, then you must rely on A.A itself for this support, in the persons of the family members who attend open meetings, and to whom you can turn for understanding and help.

If necessary, leave your husband. No one else can tell you when or whether this should be done. But don't threaten to leave and then not carry it out. In fact, try not to threaten it at all, but if you have to, simply do it.

If your husband shows any faint interest in information about alcoholism, or in any method of treatment, or recovery program, let him take the initiative about it —don't steal his show. Even if he has to go to a hospital, let him make the arrangements if he is remotely capable of it. In other words, don't treat your husband like a delinquent child, even though he may sometimes act like one. Remember that when he is sober, and even sometimes when he is drinking but not yet drunk, he is as sane as you are, and his reactions are those of an intelligent adult. At such times he can be maddened into frightful and frightening behavior by such treatment. There are, however, also times when he may appear perfectly sober, but when his mind is already drunk, so that his reactions are not quite sane. This, however, rarely happens until alcoholics have reached the last stage of their alcoholism.

Your handling of your alcoholic will, of course, differ according to the stage of alcoholism he is in. In the early stages, it is necessary to be much more wary and discreet, but at the same time it is much more possible to hold reasonable discussions (always providing they are objective and do not point the finger at him) about both drinking and alcoholism. Also he is more likely to read material you may bring home, openly, and to talk about it, since at this stage he is not so sure that "it means him." In the middle stages you can indicate much more strongly that you know he is very sick; and in the late stages you will probably have to act out this knowledge of his extreme illness constantly. At this last stage, too, you may have to take the initiative for him, although even now it is better to let him do it if he can.

It is never wise to attempt to talk seriously to an alcoholic when he is actually drunk, not even when he is drunk in a way which almost appears to be sober. His mind is not functioning normally, and therefore he is not responsible for what he says or promises; furthermore he often does not remember it, and does not believe you when you tell him what he said. The best time to talk to him is when he has a hangover: his resistance is down, his remorse is so great he is at that moment willing to do anything in order to prevent a repetition of such suffering (and of what he remembers of his drunken behavior), and for the moment he often sees clearly the steep descent of the road he is on. His self-loathing, too, is at a high pitch; so do not castigate him since you couldn't possibly do as good a job as he is inwardly doing anyway; but try and help him realize that he, as a personality and a character, is not responsible for all this: that it is all the symptoms of a vicious and terrible disease, from which he can recover if he will. If you, his wife, are the one to first lift in this way the heavy burden of guilt he has carried for so long, you will have made a great breach in the wall he has built up against the outside nonalcoholic world. He may feel for the first time that *someone* understands him, and what he is suffering, and this will be particularly important because you are his wife; it may put you in a position to help him more than anyone else, no matter what method of recovery he finally attempts.

This brings us to the final piece of advice to wives of alcoholics. *Do not feel, or act, jealous of the method of recovery he has chosen.* Do not feel that your love should have been enough to keep him from drinking, or that he should have been able to do something about his drinking *just* on account of you, and, possibly, the children. Remember always that this is not so; that you would not expect to be either the sole reason for, or the means of, his recovery from any other disease; nor would you be likely to resent the doctor, or anyone else who was helping him to recover from other illness, nor the things he might have to do in order to follow that doctor's, or individual's, or group's, suggestions. This piece of advice, of course, assumes that he has started on some program of recovery, and it includes one more don't.

Don't expect him to recover instantaneously. He may stop drinking instantaneously, but just stopping drinking is NOT recovery from alcoholism. He has a very long road to go before he arrives at full recovery, and he needs co-operation, understanding, and help all the way. Remember that it probably took him a good many years to reach the point of alcoholism which finally drove him to take action about it—he will require a number of years to fully recover, even though he may not take a single drink during those years. Incidentally, if he does drink again, remember that people have relapses during recovery from other illnesses, too; and that a relapse, or even several, does not mean they will never recover. Relapses are not to be taken lightly; they are serious setbacks, of course, to be avoided in every way possible. Fortunately a great many alcoholics never relapse once they have taken the decisive step of starting treatment; others do, however, and still make equally good and final recoveries. If you will work along with him, bearing in mind that he is struggling up a hard and rocky road of convalescence, your rewards will be great indeed. For the average alcoholic is overflowing with gratitude for the help he has received and is receiving, once his recovery has begun.

If You Are the Husband

The husband of an alcoholic has a much harder role to play than the wife of an alcoholic. More often than not, it is true, he refuses to play it, and walks out on the alcoholic wife fairly early in the game. It is a curious fact that the great majority of men who recover through Alcoholics Anonymous still have their wives; but the great majority of women (who make up, roughly, one sixth of the membership) have been divorced, some of them several times. There are comparatively few members of A.A. who have never married, and an almost equally small minority who are not married at the time they become members. This fact is contrary to a great deal of the published material on alcoholics and their marriage rates; but the number of A.A. members who have been divorced at least once bears out the published material to a certain extent, at least among the women members.

Most of the advice given to wives also applies to husbands of alcoholics. There are, however, certain differences. For instance, it is possible for a married woman alcoholic to get away with her alcoholic drinking for a much longer time without her husband realizing its extent. Particularly if he travels at all, or even if he has to spend occasional evenings away from home on business, or if he has certain evenings on which he "goes out with the boys," or plays cards away from home, she may be able for a considerable time, to confine her really uncontrolled drinking to those weeks or evenings. Sometimes, too, she will do most of her drinking during the day, and plead a headache or some other illness to account for her slightly peculiar behavior, or for her being "sick in bed" when he comes home. This, of course, cannot go very much beyond the early stages of alcoholism; fairly soon after she has reached the middle stage, the truth will become apparent. Yet it is amazing how some women alcoholics have managed to conceal the truth about their drinking from their husbands right into the last, hopelessly obvious stage. And from their friends, even then. Such women, of course, are known as chronic sufferers from "sick headaches," or neuritis or neuralgia, or some other ailment which accounts for their frequent stays in their rooms, or actually in bed.

Women alcoholics also *apparently* drink quite differently from men, in that they are not usually "convivial drinkers," rarely are bar drinkers, and quite often do not drink at all when out on parties, or in company. Instead, they are frequently solitary drinkers from the very beginning. I personally do not believe, however, that this is due to some peculiar difference in the kind of alcoholism women are subject to, or that it is actually any different from the alcoholism of men. It seems much more likely that these peculiarities are inherent in the double standard which exists for what is acceptable in women's as opposed to men's behavior. It is still not *as* acceptable for women to drink (at least more than one cocktail, or one highball, or preferably sherry or other wine) as it is for men. And it is nowhere acceptable for women to drink to drunkenness. In the hardest-drinking circles, the very men, *and women, too*, who drink the most, often make the remark, "If there's one thing I can't stand, it's to see a *woman* really *drunk*." This remark has often been made by men who are alcoholics, both active and recovered; and even by women who are recovered alcoholics, albeit with a deep and different feeling behind the remark. Despite all this, there are some women alcoholics whose drinking pattern is identical to the men's, particularly in the big cities, and among women who work.

The husband of an alcoholic woman must always remember, however, that because of this double standard, this near-universal public opinion, the guilt and shame and fear of an alcoholic wife are tenfold those of an alcoholic husband. So his approach must be even more delicate and reassuring; his stress on the disease nature of alcoholism even stronger; and his sympathetic understanding, his affectionate desire only to be of help, and the steadfastness of his love despite the unpleasant ravages of her disease made ten times more clear.

Where there are children there is an added problem of her intolerable guilt as an "unnatural mother." In order to really help her, it is sometimes necessary to send the children away. At other times they can help, too, by being made to understand that mother is really sick, suffering from a very serious disease which accounts for her strange behavior. This last fact—that her (or his) condition is due to an illness—should always be made crystal clear to the children of an alcoholic, whether it be mother or father; it may save them many neurotic twists in later life, and it is bound to save them much suffering and immediate unpleasantness. They are quite capable of understanding this, too, at a much earlier age than many people realize: as early as three or four.

If there are no children, the problem is easier in some respects, more difficult in others. For the childless woman alcoholic who is married and does not work is too often at loose ends without enough to occupy her. And it is difficult for the husband who must go to work, to take advantage of her hangover periods to try gently to bring her to constructive action. He may only see her drunk, or nearly so, for weeks on end, and she will be still "sleeping it off" when he leaves for work. Weekends are his best hope, or the occasional evenings when she drank little or nothing at all during the day. But if she ever wakes him in the night, begging for help, as happened in the movie *Smash-Up* (which gave a pretty accurate picture of a woman alcoholic), he must be prepared with knowledge and a plan of action, and he must be willing to give up his night's sleep *gladly*, in order to work out *with her* their joint attack on her problem.

Perhaps the major piece of advice to husbands of alcoholics is this: If you love your wife, despite her alcoholism, and stay with her, do it wholly and sincerely. Don't stay with her and let her feel your regret at your action, or your pulling at the restraint it makes on you, or the toll it takes on your efficiency at your work. Let her only feel the love that holds you there, and convince her that that love is solidly behind her in any action she may take regarding her condition. Make her *know* that you believe her to be the unwilling victim of a dangerous disease, and that you stand ready to help her in any way you can. Make her know that you are "with her against the world," unless and until that world comes to understand the nature of her ailment as you do.

If You Are the Son or Daughter

The children of alcoholics have frequently been the first to be able to break through the wall of resistance to the nonalcoholic world. There are countless instances of twelve- or fourteen-year-olds directly approaching their alcoholic mothers or fathers, sometimes without anything constructive to offer, save a plea to "quit"; but often, of late, with the wonderful news that they have found an answer. In the latter case, they have usually made friends at school, or camp, or in the neighborhood, with someone whose mother or father is already a member of A.A., and have learned all about it and about what to do. This has also happened in cities where there are Information Centers and/or clincs, and particularly where a local committee has managed to introduce some modern teaching about alcoholism into the schools. There is a famous case on record at one of the alcoholic clinics, where an eleven-year-old boy telephoned the clinic, and requested that they arrange for an ambulance to take both his mother and father to the hospital; he had long since learned all about alcoholism, and all there was to know about local facilities for treatment, but had had to wait to take his own action until they were both "passed out," since he had not up to that time been able to persuade them to take action of their own. They both attended the clinic as patients when they got out of the hospital, and made good recoveries.

It is not likely, however, that many children will read this book. The advice here, therefore, will be directed at adolescent and young adult children of alcoholics. The role of son or daughter gives you a great advantage in approaching an alcoholic: you can afford to be much more direct than anyone else without fear of slamming the door on any further efforts. Your pressure can be very strong, and you can hammer the point of your mother's or father's responsibilities in the case of their own serious illness, whether it be alcoholism or anything else, but particularly in the case of alcoholism because of the effect on you and your social life. You can threaten to leave home—but not without carrying out your threat—perhaps returning from a friend's or from your grandparents' for another try. Apart from these differences, your approach should include both the generai rules and the specific advice for wives and husbands.

If You Are a Friend

You will not, of course, have the same myriad opportunities to bring pressure on your alcoholic friend that a wife, husband, or child would have. Nevertheless, when opportunity offers, you can use many of the same techniques. And there is one particular technique, perhaps the most valuable of all, that you are in a better position than anyone else to use. This is the matter of instigating general discussions of drinking and alcoholism, in order to get across to the alcoholic the information you have gained on the subject, and to let him apply as much of it as he is willing or able to apply to himself. He is much more likely to make admissions about his drinking and his own concern over it to you than to his wife. And it is much more likely that you would have known other alcoholics, and what they did or didn't do about their condition, from which you can draw endless comparisons and suggest examples to follow.

Never be afraid to bring the subject up, providing you do not throw it at his head, and make him feel you are lecturing him, or condemning him. If you can remain completely objective (and this should be very much easier for you, both in actuality and to his mind, than in the case of wife, husband or child), you should be able to arouse his intense interest, and he should be able to show that interest freely to you. You are actually, therefore, in a better position than anyone to teach and inform him about his illness, and to outline constructive programs of action to him.

As a friend, too, you are in a splendid position to introduce him, without in any way raising his suspicions that you are setting a trap for him, to a recovered alcoholic who can help him, directly and personally, particularly if the alcoholic recovered through A.A. You do not always need to tell him why you are making this introduction; although if you have managed a few general conversations about drinking and alcoholism, there is no reason why you should not suggest that he might be interested in meeting and talking to so-and-so, who knows much more than you do about it, and has fascinating and interesting tales to tell. This last is always generally true for anyone, but is especially true for an alcoholic, for he is actually deeply curious and interested in the subject of drinking, if only you can break through the resistance caused by his fears that you are going to "interfere" with his drinking before he wants you to.

Sometimes it is necessary for friends who are truly friends, and do not wish to desert their alcoholic friend, to temporarily cut him out of their lives. This should never be done without having tried all other methods first, or without telling him exactly why it has become necessary, and also assuring him that it is only temporary, until he decides to do something about himself. A half measure has also occasionally been successful, in which friends have merely refused to drink with an alcoholic, but will see him on nondrinking occasions. There is no reason to fear that such actions will lose his friendship forever; it will be lost anyway if he continues untreated in his alcoholism, and if he begins a recovery program he will be grateful to you.

If You Are the Employer

The term "employer" in this case refers to anyone who holds a superior position, in office, shop, or factory, to an alcoholic employee. It can also, of course, refer to the head of the firm or company. But the person who first realizes that an employee may be an alcoholic is usually his immediate superior, who is made painfully aware of the outstanding characteristic of alcoholics in their work: unreliability. The alcoholic may be his most prized executive, his "brightest young man," who is being groomed for the top job in the business; or he may be his most productive salesman, or his top foreman, or his most highly skilled and technically proficient worker; or he may be just an ordinary worker, but steady and sound until recently, and often the best-liked man in the place. Gradually it becomes apparent that the alcoholic is changing: at first an increasing irritability and shortness of temper over office or shop affairs becomes noticeable; then unaccountable absences, or a remarkable number of "colds," or other minor indispositions which keep him away from work, begin to show. It may be quite some time before the employer realizes that drinking has anything at all to do with these manifestations, unless he happens to see a good deal of the alcoholic outside of working hours; in other words, to be a friend as well.

As soon as the employer notices any signs which could possibly mean alcoholism, he should try to do something about it. In big industries the suspected alcoholic should be sent to the medical department for a checkup, after the superior has had a frank talk with the doctors there, so that the alcoholic cannot minimize or explain away the whole thing. In smaller businesses, which do not have medical departments, the employee should be urged to consult his own doctor, and if at all possible, the information behind this urging should be conveyed to that doctor. It is unfortunately true that there are still many doctors who know little or nothing about alcoholism, and, still more unfortunately, some who do not want to know. So actually, at this stage of knowledge about alcoholism, the employer would do well to learn a little about it himself (it can't do him any harm to know, in any case!). He may then be able to act the part of a friend to his employee, even though he may not know him outside the shop or office, at all.

The major piece of advice is NOT to wait until the situation has reached such a point that the only thing to do is warn the alcoholic that he will lose his job if "it" happens again; or until still later, when the only thing to do is to fire him. The attitude of employers about alcoholism should not differ from their attitude about other illnesses, and few employers in these enlightened times fire a man because he is sick; they at least try to help him do something about his illness, first.

The employer, of course, need not take such delicate care in broaching the subject to his alcoholic employee, as wife, children and friends have to do. He is in a position to speak bluntly and to the point, and for him, this is the best way to handle it, providing he does not wait and do this at the same time he finally fires the alcoholic. The time for him to do it is while the alcoholic is still a valuable employee, while he is still functioning fairly well, and producing only a little less than his best in his job. If all employers, or job superiors, would take this advice, and add it to the general rules given here, a tremendous jump ahead could be given to our efforts to control alcoholism. Furthermore, they would be saving themselves and their businesses an incalculable sum of money, for the losses to business through alcoholism are astronomical.

On the other hand, the gains to be made from employing a recovered alcoholic are very great. Most alcoholics are good workers, whatever their line of work. It is worth good money to hold off firing an alcoholic in favor of another chance—*after* a straight talk to him about his condition and its dangers. It is worth even more to hold off firing an alcoholic if that talk produces results, and he recovers. His gratitude to the employer who helped him will be enormous, and his loyalty from then on will be way beyond the "call of duty," as will his desire to produce for the man who stood by him in his great need. The employer may need to have more than one talk with him, for the alcoholic may not take action that is immediately productive of complete sobriety; but there should not be more than three or four such talks, for if they have not produced results by then, something more drastic is needed, and the loss of the alcoholic's job may be called for.

Fortunately, industry is coming to realize the enormous stake it has in constructive action on alcoholism. This new interest is shared by both management and organized labor, to the mutual advantage of both. A number of big industries have instituted their own alcoholism programs; many more have joined in the community program, supporting and participating in the local committee on alcoholism, and then utilizing its facilities: the Alcoholism Information Center, and clinical facilities when they come into being. Two major industries have actually been the initiators of local committees on alcoholism in their communities, recognizing the direct benefits to them of a total community program. This kind of enlightened self-interest, coupled with a humanitarian concern for the well-being of both their employees and of the community in which they live, marks the recognition by American business of the importance to all of us of alcoholism and its victims, and our responsibility to do something about it.

14

WHAT THE ALCOHOLIC CAN DO HIMSELF

What everyone who knows an alcoholic should do, it ought now to be perfectly clear, is to try by every method he can devise, to bring the alcoholic to do something himself. For, as a matter of fact, only the alcoholic himself *can* do anything in the long run. But it also should be obvious from all of the foregoing, that the nonalcoholic world can do much to bring him to this point; that in fact the world has the power to persuade or prevent his taking action; and this rests a heavy responsibility on its shoulders. But this power is limited, and the old adage remains perfectly true that "you can lead a horse to water, but you can't make him drink."

One of the biggest problems is the alcoholic's own difficulty in accepting the facts about his condition. This is similar to difficulties experienced by the victims of many other diseases, notably cancer, and, to a lesser extent, diabetes. As in these and all other illnesses to which man is heir, complete acceptance by the sufferer of the truth about his condition is an essential pre-requisite to treatment and recovery. There are actually very few illnesses in which the co-operation of the patient is not a basic essential, without which nothing very much can be done. In the final analysis this is true of any and every ailment, however minor, or crucial, for if the patient does not possess the "will to live" he can die of a simple sore throat, or finger prick . . . and occasionally does.

The major factor in preventing the alcoholic from accepting the fact that he is an alcoholic, is shame. Added to this, and almost equally important, are fears of several sorts: the fear that he cannot live without alcohol, which has become the central pivot around which his life revolves; the fear of being thought "different" because he cannot do what most everyone he knows can do, and does do regularly—drink normally without in-evitably disastrous effects; the fear that he will be cut off from the pleasures of mixing with people who can drink normally, since (he thinks) they will eye him askance, and will feel uncomfortable drinking in his presence, while he will feel even more uncomfortable and as conspicuous as a sore thumb, if he refuses to drink with them. Perhaps the most virulent fear of all is the fear of being thought, or called, a weakling, and looked down upon with contempt for this weakness. This is matched only by the fear of being ridiculed.

A separate but quite devastating fear, isolated from the others because it is so deeply buried, so rarely ad-mitted, is the alcoholic's fear that he is really insane. Let it be emphasized that the people who live with this fear are average people, with the average lack of knowledge about mental illness and its ramifications. The word "insane" is a fearful word to them, carrying associations of locks and bars, strait jackets and binding sheets, and screaming contorted victims. Current public education about mental illness and its treatment should do much to alleviate the violence of this fear, perhaps one day to remove it entirely.

There is sound reasoning, and often the bitterness of past experiences, too, behind this shame and all the fears. The nonalcoholic world is gravely to blame for most of it, and must bear a great share of the responsibility for its own present difficulties in reaching and helping alcoholics; in other words, the problem of getting them to help themselves. But there are no valid reasons for such shame, or for such fears, to continue, once an alcoholic has learned the facts about alcoholism. There should be no shame in modern times for being the victim of a disease; that supposedly was left behind in the Middle Ages. There should be no shame for past behavior, *provided he is doing his best to get help to prevent its repetition,* for such behavior was symptomatic of his illness. There are other illnesses, too, which have singularly unpleasant symptoms, behavior which makes the victim feel equally shamed and humiliated unless and until he understands its real causes, and begins to do something about it. (Brain tumor, for instance, is an affliction which causes appalling behavior symptoms; and there are curable mental and nervous disturbances which do the same.)

Each one of the fears can also be eliminated through knowledge, perhaps not instantaneously, but certainly little by little. The fear of being unable to live a bearable life without drinking can be utterly wiped out by a look at, and some conversation with, a few recovered alcoholics, whom, incidentally, the alcoholic will be forced to believe since they have been through identical experiences and emotional reactions. He can even be convinced by such a person that he will begin to enjoy life, without a drop to drink, in a way he had never believed possible, surpassing his most rosy and nostalgic memories of carefree good times.

The fear of being thought "different" can be eliminated in several ways at once. First, the alcoholic must allow himself to realize the obvious fact that most people are "different" from one another in one way or another; and that perhaps the closest analogy to his own "difference" lies in diabetes, with the allergies running a close second. Most alcoholics have known someone who had an allergy: who could not eat seafood, or strawberries, or be near a dog or a horse. Second, he must learn to recognize the fact that other people do not really care what his particular "difference" may be; that in actuality they are far too preoccupied with their own, whatever that may be (and it is bound to be something, with everybody).

The fear that he will be cut off from normal drinking society is perhaps the hardest to overcome, because while an alcoholic is undergoing treatment, and often engaging in a struggle to the death with his overwhelming urge to drink, he can rarely stand being around people who are drinking happily and easily, with no fears of untoward results. For this particular fear, membership in Alcoholics Anonymous offers the only complete solution, for it automatically provides a nondrinking society in which the alcoholic has an immediate place; and the new member is frequently too busy with his new A.A. activities to find time to see his drinking friends. Later, when he is firmly set in his new pattern of nondrinking, he will be able to mix freely with drinking groups, and enjoy it, without giving a thought to taking an alcoholic drink himself. But if the alcoholic chooses another method of recovery, he may have a real problem here, for this particular fear is a real one, based on fact, not fancy. In this case, the normal drinking world in which he moves has a tremendous responsibility toward him, and must try to help him not to feel cut off and "different," at the same time without letting him feel conspicuous and humiliated because he cannot share this activity with them. They must also take care, in such a case, not to avoid him because he is *not* drinking, and not to leave him out of activities which he used to share; for this is more apt to drive him back to drinking than watching them enjoy what he cannot do.

The alcoholic himself can greatly reduce his own fear of being thought, or called, a "weakling," or spoken of as a person with a "weakness" (a word most alcoholics loathe beyond endurance). His own conviction that his trouble is a specific disease will be of the most help to him here; and if he knows any scientific facts to substantiate his conviction, he can make himself feel perfectly confident that his knowledge is superior to the ignorance of those who use such terms. There is no better way to overcome a fear, than to turn it thus into a feeling of self-confidence. Some people have raised the question as to whether teaching an alcoholic that his drinking is an illness will not give him a heavy weapon to use against those who are trying to persuade him to stop that drinking; saying that he might then be able to shrug the whole thing off with some statement like "How can I help it—it's a disease, isn't it?" or "You must let me do as I please—I'm a sick man and I can't help being like this." Actually, there are no known examples of this result of such teaching. Those who raise the question have forgotten that alcoholics, almost if not entirely without exception, spend their time trying to drink "like other people," *not* trying to drink alcoholically. They rarely want to drink the way they inevitably end up drinking. There are, of course, some exceptions who drink for oblivion, and for that only: in these cases, there may be a further problem beyond alcoholism: perhaps they are serious neurotics, in some cases even psychotics, and if so, they desperately need psychiatric help, regardless of what method they use to overcome their alcoholism.

The fear of being ridiculed can be overcome by the same method of turning the fear into self-confidence. People who ridicule an alcoholic for being unable to drink the way they themselves can drink are not only stupid, but cruel; they are, frankly, not worth the time or thought of an alcoholic or anyone else. Sometimes, of course, such behavior can be merely thoughtlessness; but it is such dangerous and cruel thoughtlessness that there are no words to excuse it. When it comes from supposedly intelligent adults, it might be well to look further into their lives and their characters: they may be dangerous people for any decent person to know, alcoholic or otherwise.

The fear of insanity can also be overcome by the development of the alcoholic's own conviction that he is suffering from an identifiable disease with a name of its own: alcoholism. The fact that there are special facilities for information about this disease, also bearing its name: Alcoholism Information and Consultation Centers; and special diagnostic and treatment clinics known as Alcoholism Clinics, is of great importance to him, helping to quiet his fear, and so enabling him to ask for help.

To learn these methods of overcoming his own shame and fear, the alcoholic must find sources of good sound information, since knowledge has been shown to be his greatest weapon. For the alcoholic, attending A.A. meetings is the simplest and most direct way of acquiring such knowledge; but he may not be willing or able to do this. It is, however, quite possible for him to obtain such information from the National Council on Alcoholism, or any of its local committees' Information Centers, and he need fear no direct "attack" on him as a result of asking for it; he will be treated like any other individual who requests information; he will be given exactly what he asks for, and no more.

It is vitally important for the alcoholic, just as it is for the wife, husband, or children of an alcoholic, to talk to someone about his problem. If he is ever to begin solving it, he must start making a hole in the prison he has built around himself. Whom he chooses to talk to is a very individual matter: his own doctor, or a doctor he has heard about who knows about alcoholism, is probably the best choice. A minister or priest can be a good choice, depending on their knowledge of alcoholism: there are many today, both Protestant and Catholic, who know a great deal, either from working closely with A.A., or from having attended the Yale Summer School of Alcohol Studies, or both. A social worker can be a good choice, particularly if the alcoholic happens to know one personally; or a psychologist or trained counsellor. Many, however, prefer to talk to a friend whom they can trust; some even talk to members of their own family. The point is, they must talk to someone: it is an absolute necessity for their own sake, for their burden is too great to be borne alone, and far too many alcoholics have committed suicide when that burden became unbearable. If they know another alcoholic who has recovered, or made a start at recovery, that is obviously the best of all.

If anyone who is an alcoholic, or who suspects he may be one, has read this book, he knows that he requires help; that he cannot hope to solve his problem alone, except in the rarest cases. He should also know that the sooner he seeks help the better for him, not to mention those whom he loves. Furthermore, he has learned where that help may be found. And finally, he has learned that, in the final analysis, it is up to him, and to no one else.

15

LET'S GO!

Everything indicates that the problem of alcoholism is going to be tackled on all fronts in the next few years. This inevitable progress can be both hastened and augmented by each and every one of us. Public opinion is nothing more than the aggregate collection of opinions like yours and mine: WE ARE PUBLIC OPINION. Therefore each one of us who learns the facts, and adopts an attitude in keeping with those facts, is making a very real contribution. If, in addition, we share our new knowledge and understanding with our friends and acquaintances, we are greatly increasing that contribution and directly helping to bring millions of suffering human beings back to health and happiness.

The world is waiting for the next move forward. One by one the diseases of mankind have been pulled out of the limbo of superstition, fear and ignorance, into the light of modern knowledge and techniques that could deal with them. One by one the scourges of man have been brought under control. We are late with alcoholism—very late—but we have the tools and we can lick it, too. It needs only our determination, as individuals, as communities, and as a nation.

The tools are available—to you—through your own national voluntary organization: the National Council on Alcoholism. If your community does not yet have a program, the plans for instituting one are ready, plus advice, guidance and assistance in carrying them out. There is no question that much more can be accomplished by an organized group than by any number of individuals working alone. If there is already a committee on alcoholism in your area, get behind it, support it, join it if you will.

Give your support to the National Council on Alcoholism too. It deserves your financial and your moral support. Contributions are deductible from your income tax! If every person in the United States who knew an alcoholic would give just one dollar *every year*, NCA's triple-attack of education, research and services could reach into every nook and cranny of this great country. NCA's program depends on you.

The main job today is devoted to securing better application of existing knowledge. That is the purpose of this book. But we must also seek to add to existing knowledge by research. Research requires money—but even more it requires public interest in a given subject, public demand for more knowledge, and public support of the search for that knowledge. Not just financial support, but the kind of moral support that will induce bright young researchers to enter the field. Researchers are people, too, and they want to work in an area where there is lively interest on the part of the public, and scientific interest among their colleagues. All of us can help to bring that about.

We can do something about prevention, too, although not as much as we might like. Prevention, in most diseases, depends primarily on education. In order to stay well and to avoid certain illnesses, we learn enough about them to protect ourselves. In some cases we don't yet know enough to be able to protect ourselves completely; we can only learn the early symptoms so that we may seek treatment at the earliest possible moment. Cancer, arthritis, diabetes, and a host of other ills are in this category. So is alcoholism. We just don't know enough, yet, to be able to predict which ones, in a classroom of children, will grow up to be alcoholics; we do know that by the law of averages, some of them will. Others will develop cancer, others diabetes, etc. All that we can do in any of these cases is to teach the children what is known about these diseases, and what to do if they ever suspect that they are showing symptoms of any one of them. This, too, can be done in the case of alcoholism. Modern teaching in the schools, based on scientific facts, must therefore be a major goal of any alcoholism program.

In all of this YOU can help. "Many hands make light work" is particularly true in alcoholism. Your hands are needed—and your heads—and your hearts. LET'S GO!

SELECTED BIBLIOGRAPHY

Alcohol Explored, Haggard and Jellinek, Doubleday, 1942

Alcohol—One Man's Meat, Strecker & Chambers, Macmillan, 1938

"Alcohol, Science and Society" (29 lectures), *Quarterly Journal of Studies on Alcohol*, New Haven, Conn., 1945

Alcohol and Social Responsibility, McCarthy & Douglass, Crowell, 1949

Alcoholics Anonymous, A.A. Publishing, Inc., 1955

Alcoholics Anonymous Comes of Age, A.A. Publishing, Inc. and Harper & Brothers, 1957

Alcoholism, Arnold Z. Pfeffer, M.D., Grune & Stratton, 1958.

Alcoholism, Its Scope, Cause, and Treatment, Ruth Fox, M.D., and Peter Lyon, Random House, 1955

Depth Psychology, Morality and Alcoholism, Rev. J. C. Ford, S.J., Weston College, Weston, Mass., 1951

Hope and Help for the Alcoholic, H. W. Lovell, M.D., Doubleday, 1956

How to Live Without Liquor, Ralph A. Habas, Ph.D., Farrar, Strauss and Cudahy, 1955

Just One More, James L. Free, Coward-McCann, 1955

Man Takes a Drink, Rev. J. C. Ford, S.J., P. J. Kenedy & Sons, 1955

Quarterly Journal of Studies on Alcohol, Box 2162, Yale Station, New Haven, Conn.

The Treatment of the Alcoholic, Fritz Kant, M.D., Charles C. Thomas, Springfield, Ill., 1954

Understanding and Counseling the Alcoholic Through Religion and Psychiatry, Rev. H. J. Clinebell, Jr., Abingdon Press, 1956